GETTING READY TO CHANGE THE WORLD

— NEW CHALLENGES, NEW OPPORTUNITIES —

グローバル時代を生き抜く変革への視点

FRANÇOIS DE SOETE

JN062922

SEIBIDO

著者紹介

Dr. François de Soete（政治学博士）

アリゾナ州立大学にて歴史学および政治学の2つの学士号を最優秀で修めたのち、ブリティッシュ・コロンビア大学大学院にて政治学の修士号と博士号を取得。日本および北米の大学で政治哲学や国際関係論の授業を担当し、学術論文の執筆や国際学会における発表を行ってきた。本書は、『民主主義の歩みと現代国家』（2012年）、『現代世界を理解するための視点』（2014年）、『グローバル社会を読み解く新たな視点』（2017年）に続く成美堂からの4冊目の教科書。

About the Author

Dr. François de Soete graduated summa cum laude from Arizona State University, where he received a B.A. in political science and a B.A. in history. He then pursued his graduate studies at the University of British Columbia, where he earned an M.A. and a Ph.D. in political science. He has taught university courses on political philosophy and international relations in Japan and North America, and has published research articles and presented papers at academic conferences on these topics. This is now his fourth textbook with Seibido, the prior three being: *Democracy Around the World: Ancient Origins and Contemporary Practices* (2012), *Making Sense of the World: Wisdom Through Knowledge* (2014), and *Thinking About Our Place in the World: New Questions, New Answers* (2017).

Cover photographs by	**Photographs by**
The Author	The Author
NASA	@ iStockPhoto
	NASA
	NASA/JPL
	The White House
	National Park Service
	AP/AFLO

音声ファイルのダウンロード／ストリーミング

CDマーク表示がある箇所は、音声を弊社HPより無料でダウンロード／ストリーミングすることができます。トップページのバナーをクリックし、書籍検索してください。書籍詳細ページに音声ダウンロードアイコンがございますのでそちらから自習用音声としてご活用ください。

https://www.seibido.co.jp

Getting Ready to Change the World
—New Challenges, New Opportunities—

Copyright © 2020 by François de Soete

Preface

The only constant in life is change. This statement is often attributed to the ancient Greek philosopher Heraclitus, and given that since the dawn of the twentieth century we have witnessed change at a pace previously unseen in the history of human civilization, it is a saying that seems especially apt today. After all, in the span of just a little over a hundred years, we have gone from weeks at sea, to just hours in the air to cross oceans; from sending telegrams, to sending text messages; and from the ever-present risk of war between major powers, to largely economically interdependent countries. We have gone from a field of medicine that could not even cure a simple bacterial infection, to one where surgery deep inside the brain is possible. We have gone from the first powered flight that barely left the ground, to landing on the Moon. In short, our world has undergone an unprecedented level of change over the past century, and we may well end up experiencing an even more dramatic level of change in the coming decades.

One relatively recent change that we can already see progressing rapidly is that companies and universities are increasingly internationalizing. Most people simply do not have time to learn many different languages in order to communicate with people from various parts of the world, and so at this point in time English serves as a common second language that allows people with different linguistic backgrounds to communicate with one another. However, it is not enough to merely have the language skills needed to communicate with others, but rather, it is also important to develop informed perspectives in order to be able to communicate intelligently about a wide variety of topics. This textbook therefore features a diverse array of chapters that strike a balance between casual topics, like tourism, and more serious topics, like genetic engineering. Although each chapter includes certain technical terms, colloquial phrases, and advanced vocabulary, Hokkaido University professor emeritus Katsunosuke Namita has added numerous Japanese annotations to help readers understand these terms and phrases. Having had the opportunity to once again work with Professor Namita was a great pleasure, and as this now marks the fourth time that we have collaborated on a textbook for Seibido, it is important to note that his tireless efforts on this latest book are immensely appreciated.

While only a few notable people may have the power to profoundly transform the world, each and every person will nevertheless have at least some small impact on the world in which we live. This book therefore aims to impart the kind of knowledge and language skills that can prove useful to readers, who are, whether they realize it or not, getting ready to change the world.

François de Soete

はしがき

　この世で唯一不変のものは変化である（万物は流転する）。これはギリシャの哲学者ヘラクレイトスの言葉である。20世紀の初めから、人類の文明史においてこれまで類を見ないほどの速さで変化するのを目の当たりにしてきたことを考えると、この格言はとりわけ今日にふさわしいと言える。わずか100年ちょっとの間に、大洋を渡るのに海上を何週間もかけていたのが、空中をわずか数時間で飛び越えるようになり、電報を送っていたのが、テキストメッセージを送るようになり、大国間で戦争勃発の危機が絶えず存在していたのが、主として経済的に相互依存する関係へと変化した。医療分野においても、単なる細菌感染さえ治療することができなかったのが、脳の深部における手術も可能になった。地面からわずかに浮き上がったかどうかという初の動力飛行から、月面着陸まで達成した。要するに、私たちの世界はこの100年の間にかつてないほどの変化を経験し、次の数十年間でさらに飛躍的な変化が待ち受けているかもしれないのだ。

　比較的最近、急速に進んでいることが目に見える変化の１つは、企業や大学がますます国際化している点だ。多くの人は世界各国の人々とコミュニケーションを取るためにいくつもの言語を習得する時間がないので、現時点では言語が異なる人々が互いに意思疎通を図る際には英語が共通の第２言語として用いられている。しかしながら、単に語学力があるだけでは不十分で、様々な話題に関して知的なコミュニケーションを取るためには、確かな情報に基づいたものの見方を養うことが大事である。従って本書は、観光のような身近なテーマから遺伝子工学などの重い内容まで、多様なトピックをバランスよく扱っている点が特徴である。各章には専門用語やくだけた表現、上級の語彙が含まれることもあるが、読者の皆さんが理解しやすいように、北海道大学名誉教授の浪田克之介先生が丁寧に注釈を付けてくださっている。浪田先生と再び一緒に仕事ができたことは大変光栄であった。成美堂の教科書に共同で取り組むのはこれが4冊目であるが、本書の刊行に当たっても多大なご尽力をいただいたことに、感謝の気持ちを述べたい。

　世界を劇的に変える力を持っているのはごくわずかの著名人だけかもしれないが、社会を構成している人々の誰もがこの社会に何らかの影響を与えている。従って、自ら意識しているかどうかにかかわらず、世界を変える準備をしつつある皆さんに、本書で有用な知識や語学力を身に付けてもらえれば幸いである。

　最後に、本書の企画・編集に当たりお世話になった成美堂編集部の佐藤公雄氏に謝意を表したい。

François de Soete

本書の使い方

各章の構成は以下の通りとなっている。

導入文

各章の冒頭に、本文のトピックに関する簡単な導入説明や問いかけが日本語で書かれている。学生にとってこれまであまりなじみのないテーマであったとしても、この導入文を読むことで興味関心をもってリーディングに取り組むことができる。

Getting Started

本文を読み始める前に、その準備として関連内容について学生が自分で考えることのできる質問を3つ用意してある。個人の意見や体験を問うものであるので、下調べの必要はない。一文で答えを書くよう指示してあるが、授業内でディスカッションの題材として利用することも可能である。

Reading

明快な英文で書かれた本文は、文化、社会、メディア、自然科学、テクノロジーなど多様で身近なトピックを扱っている。予備知識がなくても、本文を読めば十分に理解できる内容となっている。また、基本的には5000語レベル以上の単語や固有名詞に注釈を付けている。

Vocabulary

本文で使用された単語の意味を選択する問題。知らない単語であっても、辞書を使うのではなく、文中で使用されている箇所を読みながら解答を推測するよう指示している。単語の類義語を学習することにもつながる。

Comprehension

本文の内容理解を問う問題。本文の該当箇所を特定すれば答えられる易しい問題だけではなく、本文の内容全体と問題文の意味をよく理解していなければ解答できない難しめのものも用意してあるので、内容分析やクリティカル・リーディングの力を養うことができる。

Summary

CDを聴きながら空欄になっている単語を書き取る問題。Getting Startedの変化の聞き取りと、つづりの練習になっている。リスニングの文章は、本文全体の要旨になっており、本文の内容理解のチェックにも利用することができる。

Discussion

本文で扱うトピックに関連する質問を1つ用意してある。Getting Startedの質問と同様に、学生自身の意見や体験を問うものであり下調べは必要ないが、なぜそのように考えたのか、自分の意見を人にわかりやすく説明する形で答えるよう指示してある。ライティングあるいはディスカッションに利用できるようになっている。

Point of Interest

本文で扱っているトピックや人物に関連した、おもしろい豆知識を平易な英文で紹介したコラム。本文の関連箇所に、日本語でこの欄への参照指示が掲載されており、学生自身が関心に応じて読み進めることができる。教科書の問題や小テストなどには、このコラムの内容は含まれていないが、楽しみながら各章のテーマに関する知識や理解を広げるのに役立つ。

Table of Contents

Section I: Media and Entertainment

Section II: People and Nature

Section III: Culture and Society

Section IV: Science and Technology

Going Viral

How are some people getting so famous online?

現代では、有名性を測る基準はソーシャルメディアでどれだけのフォロワーがいるかどうかになったようだ。有名人がファンとの交流のためにソーシャルメディアを使うこともあれば、ソーシャルメディアを利用して有名になる一般人もいる。極めて多くの人がソーシャルメディアを使うこの時代に、ネットで拡散されるコンテンツを作り人気を得ている人は、一般のユーザーと何が違うのだろうか。

The desire to get great photos leads some photographers to take serious risks, like getting right next to a perilous flow of rushing water. With the rise of social media, some people are willing to do even more dangerous things to post attention-grabbing photos.

Image credit: The author

Getting Started

To help you connect with this chapter's topic, take a moment to think about the questions below, and then write a short sentence to answer each one.

1. How often do you post content on your social media accounts?

   _____

2. How many followers would you like to have on social media?

   _____

3. Approximately how many people do you follow on social media?

   _____

Reading

1 Most social media users have only a modest number of followers on their accounts, but some celebrities, sports stars, and even some politicians have millions of followers. Superstar celebrities like Katy Perry and Justin Bieber, for instance, have over a hundred million followers. The number of followers
5 celebrities have on social media largely reflects the fame they have achieved as entertainers. For others, social media serves as a ticket to fame. Sites like YouTube, Instagram, Facebook, and Twitter make it possible for anyone to attempt to become an Internet celebrity, which does not require dealing with
10 talent agencies, movie studios, or publishers. Being able to bypass the traditional route to celebrity makes it seem as though becoming a cyberstar is easy, but getting noticed online often requires creating something that goes viral—which for most people is far from easy.

> 世界中でソーシャル
> メディアを利用する
> 人はどのくらいいる
> のか、章末の Point
> of Interest を読んで
> みよう。

2 When someone uploads a video, for example, and the number of people who
15 reshare it begins to rise rapidly, we can say that this person's video is going viral. We use the expression "going viral" because the video seemingly spreads in a way that is similar to the way a highly contagious virus like influenza spreads. Basically, a few people watch the video and find it so attention-grabbing that they feel compelled to forward the video's link to their friends, and those friends forward it to their friends, and so
20 on. If a sequence such as this grows to involve thousands of people over the course of a relatively short period of time, then we can say that the video is going viral. Any type of content online, whether it is a video, an image, or something written like a blog or tweet, has the potential to go viral.

3 This raises an obvious question: why do certain things go viral while most
25 content goes largely unnoticed? Part of it comes down to one's personal traits and social media savvy. Different types of people have different traits and talents that can help them get noticed. Some people are naturally funny, for instance, and others have great
30 charisma, while some have amazing gaming skills, and others are especially insightful. If someone has particularly **appealing**[1] traits or talents, and he or she knows how to use social media effectively, then the things this person posts online are likely to get noticed
35 and reshared. Part of it also comes down to the appeal of the content itself. An old saying in journalism

Smartphones, useful social media tools
Image credit: @iStockphoto

applies here: "dog bites man" is not news, but "man bites dog" is news. In other words, commonplace events simply do not **capture**[2] anyone's attention, but unusual events do. Things that can go viral include: a really bizarre incident in public that happens to be caught on video, a controversial tweet, or a photo of an especially cute dog or cat making a funny face. In some cases, things a bit more profound go viral, like a timely 5 blog post that offers unique insight on something that affects many people, a story about something like an amazing act of generosity, or a heart-wrenching tragedy.

05 CD

4 There is unfortunately another old saying that applies to this discussion: "there is no such thing as bad publicity." Some people are willing to do things that are shocking, possibly dangerous, and maybe even illegal in order to get attention 10 online. Some risk serious injury and possibly death by doing, for example, incredibly dangerous daredevil stunts. Others do things that most people consider shocking, like eating something really disgusting. Some break the law by doing things like filming themselves driving dangerously on public roads. Some will even create situations that look real, but are actually staged, like one person pretending to surprise a friend and 15 that friend giving an over-the-top reaction. More nefariously, though, some people make up tragic stories or fabricate stories of amazing human kindness in an effort to not only go viral, but to also make money by fraudulently starting crowdfunding campaigns based on their viral content.

06 CD

5 We often read about ordinary people who start using social media, build a 20 sizeable following, monetize their social media feeds, and become rich cyberstars. These success stories entice some people to set their sights on social media as a ticket to fame, but it is important to remember that with so many people posting things online every day, it is quite difficult for the average social media user to create something that stands out and goes viral. The good news, though, is that trying to make it big on 25 social media does not require the same level of sacrifice and commitment as trying to become, for example, a movie star or a professional athlete. This means that people can **pursue**[3] full-time careers as salaried employees, and yet still spend time on social media after work in an effort to create something that ends up going viral, which could end up setting them on the path to online stardom. 30

NOTES ....

Katy Perry「ケイティ・ペリー（1984- ）米国のシンガーソングライター」 **Justin Bieber**「ジャスティン・ビーバー（1994- ）カナダの歌手・俳優」 **bypass**「無視する」 **cyberstar**「インターネット上の有名人」 **go viral**「（インターネットなどを介して）急速に拡散する」 **reshare**「再共有する」 **contagious**「感染性の」 **forward**「転送する」 **trait**「特性」 **savvy**「能力」 **post**「載せる」 **bizarre**「奇怪な」 **generosity**「気前のよさ」 **heart-wrenching**「胸を締め付けられるような」 **bad publicity**「悪評」 **daredevil**「度が過ぎた」 **disgusting**「気分が悪くなるような」 **staged**「仕組まれた」 **over-the-top**「度が超えた」 **nefariously**「極悪なまでに」 **fabricate**「作り上げる」 **fraudulently**「不正に」 **crowdfunding**「クラウドファンディング（不特定多数の人からインターネットを介して資金を集めること）」 **sizeable**「相当な」 **monetize**「（ウェブサイト

などから）広告収入を得る」 **feed**「（Web サイトの）配信情報」 **entice**「そそのかして〜させる」 **make it big**「大いに成功する」

Vocabulary

Use the context in the reading section to figure out the meaning of each underlined word below.

1. … has particularly **appealing** traits or talents …
   - a. honorable
   - b. good
   - c. artificial
   - d. attractive

2. … events simply do not **capture** anyone's attention …
   - a. catch
   - b. share
   - c. trust
   - d. decide

3. … people can **pursue** full-time careers as …
   - a. undertake
   - b. suggest
   - c. lead
   - d. persuade

Comprehension

Read each statement below carefully, and then based on the information presented in this chapter, write "T" if it is true or "F" if it is false.

1. _____ The expression "going viral" is based on the similarity between the way some things spread online and the way viruses spread.

2. _____ "Dog bites man" is an example of a unique news story that gets people's attention.

3. _____ Efforts to make videos and other social media content go viral can lead people to engage in dangerous behavior.

4. _____ Some people make up stories in an effort to go viral and get money from crowdfunding campaigns.

5. _____ According to the author, becoming a social media star is easy because there is so much content posted daily on social media.

Summary

Listen carefully to the audio recording for this section and fill in the blanks in the paragraph below.

It 1)_____ that social media has become the ultimate measure of fame, for the more followers someone has, the more famous he or she must be. While people like movie stars and professional athletes have many followers due to their celebrity status, others have 2)_____ to use social media to emerge from obscurity to become famous. For those who use social media in hopes of achieving fame, sometimes all it takes to get on the 3)_____ to fame is simply posting something that ends up going viral. In some cases people draw on their 4)_____ talents to create appealing content, but in other cases people behave irresponsibly in an effort to get noticed. Either way, with so many social media 5)_____ posting countless videos, tweets, blogs, and photos online every day, creating content that goes viral is the exception, not the norm.

Discussion

Write a short response to the question below. Be prepared to discuss your answer out loud with fellow students if your instructor asks you to do so.

What is the most recent viral content that you have seen online? Explain why you think this content went viral.

....

....

....

⊕ Point of Interest

There are literally billions of people on social media today. At the end of 2018, for example, over 2.6 billion people a month were using apps in the Facebook family, which includes Facebook, WhatsApp, Instagram, and Messenger.

Tourist Traps

How is overtourism reshaping life for locals?

今日、海外旅行は世界的なブームである。しかし観光客が旅行先で楽しんでいる一方で、地元住民にとっては必ずしも良いことばかりではない。オーバーツーリズム（観光公害）は、地元住民にどのような影響を及ぼしているのだろうか。

Small cities in Europe that serve as tourist hotspots are now actually trying to limit the number of tourists that visit. One such example is the small city of Bruges, Belgium, which is famous for its market square and its towering belfry overlooking the town.

Image credit: The author

Getting Started

To help you connect with this chapter's topic, take a moment to think about the questions below, and then write a short sentence to answer each one.

1. How many times per year do you travel by airplane?

   _____

2. How often do you encounter tourists in your home city?

   _____

3. If you could travel to any place in the world, where would you go?

   _____

Reading

1 People love to travel. Few things in life are more exciting than heading to the airport and then flying off to a distant land to see, for example, the Eiffel Tower in Paris, or to try authentic local cuisine like pho in Vietnam, or to watch a bull riding competition at the Calgary Stampede in Canada, or to go sailing along the coast of Australia. Regardless of the specifics, just about everybody who can afford it takes a trip abroad at one time or another, and in most cases, they come back with great memories that last a lifetime. While there is no denying that taking a journey to new places is typically a wonderful experience for travelers, it is not quite as clear-cut when it comes to the inhabitants of the places that tourists visit. Getting visitors from all around the world may in some ways benefit popular tourist destinations like Paris and Kyoto, but as we will see

View from an airplane window
Image credit: The author

in this chapter, the constant presence of tourists can be **disruptive**[1] for residents, and it is increasingly starting to look like many places around the world are experiencing overtourism.

2 According to the United Nations World Tourism Organization, there were a little over 1.32 billion international tourist arrivals in 2017, which marked a seven-percent increase from 2016. International tourists spent a whopping 1.34 trillion dollars in 2017, which is a five-percent increase from 2016. Needless to say, tourism is big business—it is literally a trillion-dollar industry. Much of the international tourism boom is fueled by the airline industry, which has helped connect the world in unprecedented ways. According to the International Air Transport Association, by 2017 airlines

> 航空機製造の大手2社が、近年に飛行機を何機販売したのか、章末の Point of Interest を読んでみよう。

were offering regular services to over twenty thousand city pairs, which is over twice the number of city pairs that airlines connected in 1995. Furthermore, there were 4.1 billion passenger trips by air in 2017, which is an increase of 280 million trips from 2016. Quite simply, people are on average traveling more today than ever before, and the number of people taking trips is growing.

3 International tourism is clearly good for visitors, but those who live in places that attract tourists, however, may not see much benefit. Though the tax revenue from businesses that **profit**[2] from tourism theoretically benefits a host jurisdiction as a whole, the businesses themselves profit the most, and the residents are forced to bear the difficulties that come with tourism even though they have relatively little stake in the tourism industry. For example, Venice, Italy, gets over twenty million tourists per year, yet the population is now under sixty thousand in the city itself, and so local inhabitants are often like outsiders in their own home city since there are so many tourists present at any given time. Relatively small cities like Venice are clearly affected the most by a heavy influx of visitors, but residents in large cities like London and Paris also feel the effects of tourism during the peak summer travel season. Most notably, crowding on public transportation, on the streets, and in local eateries can be a nuisance for residents who simply want to get to work, or want to have a quick meal during their lunch break.

11 🎧

4 Another problem lies in the reality that tourists and residents typically have conflicting lifestyles. Tourists are on vacation, and so they are usually inclined to go out later, and the excitement of being on vacation often puts them in a more festive mindset. This is especially problematic when they stay in apartments and houses that are rented out as short-term rentals, where neighbors are frequently residents who get up for work in the morning. Whereas neighbors typically have some degree of mutual respect when it comes to issues like noise and trash disposal, tourists are there for just a few nights and so they likely do not concern themselves much with such things. If even just a few units in an apartment building are used for this type of housing, for example, dealing with different tourists constantly coming and going throughout the year can be a nightmare for residents.

12 🎧

5 The bottom line is that the tourism industry is growing rapidly, and dealing with tourists is simply a part of life for residents who live in cities that serve as popular travel destinations. Tourism is so lucrative that many countries are actively trying to attract more and more tourists. In the case of Japan, for example, nearly twenty million foreign tourists came to visit in 2015, which was nearly double the number of tourists seen in the country in 2014. Japan had set a goal of drawing twenty million visitors per year by 2020, but given that this target was essentially already achieved in 2015, the government set a new target of forty million visitors a year by 2020, and aims to attract sixty million visitors a year by 2030. Though countries that seek to dramatically increase the number of tourists like this can reap economic benefits, some of their citizens may end up experiencing drawbacks. It is therefore **imperative**[3] that the proper infrastructure and facilities are in place in order to ensure that tourists experience all the wonders that a country has to offer, without excessively infringing on the daily life of residents.

NOTES ....

authentic「正当な」 **cuisine**「料理」 **pho**「フォー（ベトナム料理の平たい米粉麺）」 **Calgary Stampede**「カルガリー・スタンピード（カナダのカルガリー市で開催される、チャックワゴン（幌馬車）レースやロデオなどの野外ショー）」 **World Tourism Organization**「世界観光機関」 **whopping**「途方もなく大きい」 **eatery**「レストラン」 **festive**「お祭り気分の」 **mindset**「精神状態」 **lucrative**「金になる」 **reap**「得る」 **drawback**「不利益」 **fringe**「侵害する」

Vocabulary

Use the context in the reading section to figure out the meaning of each underlined word below.

1. … can be **disruptive** for residents …
   - a. exciting
   - b. tiring
   - c. boring
   - d. troublesome

2. … the businesses themselves **profit** the most …
   - a. benefit
   - b. challenge
   - c. contribute
   - d. lose

3. … therefore **imperative** that the proper …
   - a. interesting
   - b. valuable
   - c. accurate
   - d. important

Comprehension

Read each statement below carefully, and then based on the information presented in this chapter, write "T" if it is true or "F" if it is false.

1. _____ The number of international tourist arrivals and the amount of money tourists spent both increased from 2016 to 2017.

2. _____ In Venice, Italy, the local population of six million residents makes it difficult to accommodate the millions of tourists who visit every year.

3. _____ Tourists and residents typically have a different mindset, which is especially problematic with short-term rentals in apartment buildings.

4. _____ Japan already has attracted nearly twenty million tourists per year, and is aiming to draw in sixty million tourists by the year 2020.

5. _____ According to the author, the economic benefits from tourism are more important than the inconveniences to residents.

Summary

Listen carefully to the audio recording for this section and fill in the blanks in the paragraph below.

It seems like everyone loves to travel, and the booming trillion-dollar international tourism industry is evidence of just how much people enjoy taking trips ₁)_____. While it is obvious that tourists enjoy their time in other countries, a large influx of ₂)_____ is not necessarily good for those who live in places that are considered popular travel destinations. On the one hand, tourism generates a lot of ₃)_____ for the host country, which can help its economy. On the other hand, many residents have to deal with ₄)_____ during peak travel times, and having tourists staying in short-term rentals can create problems like late-night noise for some residents. The reality is that the tourism industry is growing, and so people who live in popular tourist ₅)_____ have to find ways to adapt.

Discussion

Write a short response to the question below. Be prepared to discuss your answer out loud with fellow students if your instructor asks you to do so.

What part of traveling somewhere new is the most exciting for you? Please explain your answer.

....

....

....

🌐 Point of Interest

Boeing delivered 806 commercial airplanes in 2018, which was a slight increase from the 763 it delivered in 2017, while Airbus delivered 800 aircraft in 2018, a slight increase from the 718 it delivered in 2017. To put these numbers in perspective, as of March of 2018, the Japan Airlines (JAL) Group had 231 airplanes in use. This means that these two manufacturers alone produced nearly seven times as many aircraft in 2018 as there are in the JAL Group's fleet.

Deal Me In

What makes poker tournaments so popular?

ここ数十年間で、ポーカートーナメントが人気を博すようになった。今日では、ポーカーはギャンブルというよりは、非身体的スポーツのように捉えられている。ポーカーの中で最も普及しているテキサスホールデムを通して、ポーカーの人気の秘密を探ってみよう。

A game of Texas hold 'em poker begins when the dealer deals each player two cards, which are known as a player's "hole cards." Each player must make sure to avoid letting other players know what his or her hole cards are.

Image credit: @iStockphoto

Getting Started

To help you connect with this chapter's topic, take a moment to think about the questions below, and then write a short sentence to answer each one.

1. What is your favorite game that does not involve sports or electronics?

   _____

2. How often do you play competitive games with other people?

   _____

3. Which card game seems most interesting to you?

   _____

Reading

1 Poker tournaments have become increasingly popular over the last several decades. Some tournaments host thousands of players, and some offer grand prizes worth millions of dollars. For instance, the winner of the World Series of Poker Main Event in 2018 received nearly nine million dollars, which is more than twice the
5 amount that the men's singles winner and the women's singles winner of the U.S. Open tennis tournament received in 2018, who each received a little under four million dollars. The game of poker was originally a popular, and often rough, form of gambling found in many saloons when it first developed in the United States in the nineteenth century. Today, however, poker is more like a non-physical sport than a
10 form of gambling, and as we will see in this chapter, a few of this game's key features help explain why it is so popular.

2 There are many different forms of poker, but Texas hold 'em is the most popular. A Texas hold 'em poker tournament may have just a few players filling one table, or thousands of players on multiple tables playing in elimination mode. Each
15 player must pay what is essentially an entry fee, and these payments then form the prize pool. Every player starts with the same number of playing chips, which are used to place bets. A player is eliminated when he or she runs out of chips, and the tournament ends when only one player remains. Prize money is **distributed**[1] at the end of the tournament to the top players, and so in many ways this format is similar to
20 that found in a golf or tennis tournament. Though the rules of Texas hold 'em are too numerous to list here in their entirety, an explanation of some basic features can help clarify how the game works and why so many people find it intriguing.

3 To start things off, the dealer deals each player two cards face down, so that players can only see their own two cards, which are referred to as "hole cards." The
25 dealer then deals up to an additional three rounds of cards face up, at the center of the table: three cards that are together known as "the flop," followed by a single card known as "the turn," and then one last card known as "the river." After each round, players place bets based on how they perceive their hand strength at that particular juncture in
30 the game. For instance, after they are dealt their hole cards, players must **decide**[2] whether or not they have a good chance of winning the hand. If so, they can "call," which means matching the highest bet already placed by another player, or they can "raise," which means placing a higher bet that others must match if they wish to stay in the game. If not, they can "fold," which
35 means quitting the hand and losing whatever chips they have bet so far in this hand. If at least two players remain after these bets are placed, then the dealer deals the flop

> ポーカーの初期の歴史について、章末の Point of Interest を読んで、さらに理解を深めよう。

and players go through this same decision-making process again, and once more with the turn, and yet again with the river. Once a winner for the hand is determined, the dealer deals fresh cards and a new hand begins, and this process repeats until one player has won every other player's chips.

17 CD

4 Players decide how much to bet based on how confident they are that they 5 have a winning hand. In Texas hold 'em, players **strive**[3] to create the strongest five-card

hand possible based on a combination of cards from one's own hole cards and the community cards, which are the three to five cards that make up the flop, turn, and river. For example, if someone has a two in his hole cards, and there is a three, a four, a five, and a six in the community cards, then that player can make what is called a six-high straight—five cards in numerical sequence, with the highest card being a six. However, if another player has

Hole cards in hand, community cards in the middle
Image credit: @iStockphoto

10

15

a seven and an eight as his or her hole cards, then that player can make an eight-high straight, which would win the hand since eight is higher than six. Players must 20 therefore look at their hole cards and the community cards to figure out what hand they can form, but also consider what hand other players might be able to form based on the community cards.

18 CD

5 While random chance obviously plays a role in the outcome of any given hand, three skills in particular can help offset this random chance element. First, players with 25 a good understanding of probabilities can usually make good bets more often than bad bets. Second, a player with a good "poker face" can bluff, which means getting other players to believe that he or she has a strong hand when in reality it is a weak hand, or vice versa. Third, and on a related note, players who can read other players can often tell whether or not other players are bluffing and adjust their bets accordingly. This 30 skill element can create truly dramatic finishes. For instance, when only two players remain, and one of them bets everything he or she has, the other player has to figure out: is that player bluffing, or does he or she really have the cards to back up that bet? This competitive aspect, which involves strategy, intuition, and a bit of luck, is what has helped make Texas hold 'em poker so popular—and the best part is that even those 35 who have never played before can join a tournament and take a shot at winning it all.

Texas hold 'em「テキサス・ホールデム」 elimination「敗退」 pool「掛け金」 intriguing「面白い」 hole card「ホールカード, 伏せたカード」 bet「掛け金」 juncture「形勢」 raise「より多く賭ける」 fold「伏せて卓上におく」 community card「コミュニティーカード（全てのプレーヤーに共通に使われる表向きのカード）」 offset「相殺する」 bluff「はったりをかける」

Vocabulary

Use the context in the reading section to figure out the meaning of each underlined word below.

1. … money is **distributed** at the end …
   - a. donated   b. allocated   c. generated   d. located
2. … players must **decide** whether or not …
   - a. determine   b. argue   c. illustrate   d. fabricate
3. … players **strive** to create the strongest …
   - a. attempt   b. enjoy   c. mandate   d. entice

Comprehension

Read each statement below carefully, and then based on the information presented in this chapter, write "T" if it is true or "F" if it is false.

1. _____ The winner of the 2018 World Series of Texas hold 'em poker received nearly four million dollars in prize money.

2. _____ If a player decides to "raise," it means that he or she is matching the highest bet made by another player.

3. _____ Each player must use both of his or her hole cards when playing a hand of Texas hold 'em poker.

4. _____ Player skill, according to this chapter, does not influence the outcome in Texas hold 'em since this game is based on random chance.

5. _____ The author believes that the main reason why poker is so popular is that even if players have a weak hand, they can bluff to win.

Summary

Listen carefully to the audio recording for this section and fill in the blanks in the paragraph below.

Texas hold 'em is the most popular 1)_____ of poker, and tournaments that feature this type of poker can bring in thousands of players. Players begin with a set number of chips, which they use to play during rounds of 2)_____ that eventually leave only one player standing, who is declared the tournament champion. Broadly speaking, the objective in Texas hold 'em is to 3)_____ one's hole cards and the community cards to create the strongest hand possible. However, the key to 4)_____ is to be able to deceive other players by bluffing about one's own hand strength, and to be able to recognize whether bets by other players actually reflect the strength of the cards they are holding. This aspect of the game therefore makes Texas hold 'em more than just a game of 5)_____, but one that involves strategy and intuition.

Discussion

Write a short response to the question below. Be prepared to discuss your answer out loud with fellow students if your instructor asks you to do so.

How important is it to win when you play competitive games with your friends or fellow club members? Please explain your answer.

....

....

....

🌐 Point of Interest

Poker uses what is called the French deck, which has fifty-two cards sorted into four suits: spades, clubs, diamonds, and hearts. The following list includes most of the hand types that players can form, ranked from weakest to strongest: (1) "pair," which is two cards with the same face value; (2) "two pairs;" (3) "three of a kind," which is three cards with the same face value; (4) "straight," which is five cards in sequence; (5) "flush," which is any five cards in the same suit; (6) "full house," which is three of a kind and a pair; (7) "four of a kind, which is four cards with the same face value;" (8) "straight flush," which is five cards in sequence from the same suit. The face value of cards also determines hand strength, which means that, for example, a pair of tens is stronger than a pair of fives, and a straight that ends with a nine is stronger than a straight that ends with an eight.

Full Contact

Are some sports too rough?

アメリカンフットボールやアイスホッケーなどのフルコンタクトと呼ばれるスポーツでは、試合中に選手が相手に対して激しく身体を接触することが認められている。しかし頭部を負傷すると、後遺症に悩まされたり命にかかわることもあるため、問題視されるようになってきた。プロスポーツリーグがどのような対応をしたのか見てみよう。

Many sports feature a certain degree of physical contact, but a few sports, most notably ice hockey and American football, involve such fierce hitting that some players can potentially suffer serious head injuries with lasting effects.

Image credit: @iStockphoto

Getting Started

To help you connect with this chapter's topic, take a moment to think about the questions below, and then write a short sentence to answer each one.

1. How often do you watch professional sports games?

   _____

2. What do you think of sports like ice hockey and American football?

   _____

3. What is your favorite sport to play?

   _____

Reading

1 Full-contact sports like professional American football and professional ice hockey are some of the most popular sports today. These sports routinely feature punishing hits and some brutal collisions when players run or skate full speed into each other while striving to help their team win. As famed National Football League (NFL) coach Vince Lombardi allegedly once said, "winning isn't everything, it is the only 5 thing." This sort of mindset in contact sports may have fueled the kind of hard hitting that at times caused serious head injuries, and motivated players suffering from the effects of head injuries to play through the pain. Today, however, professional sports are taking the risk of head injuries more seriously, for injuries that result in trauma to the brain have the potential to not only affect a player's athletic career, but his or her 10 regular life as well. Let us therefore take a closer look at the risk of head injuries in sports and how professional leagues have changed their approach to protecting players.

2 Punishing hits have long been part of hockey and football, and it used to be relatively commonplace to see a player receive a hard blow to the head. Until recent

changes to the rules, there were instances where a 15 player would suffer a concussion, and yet would continue playing in the game. For example, Canadian hockey player Paul Kariya was hit so hard in the head area during a National Hockey League (NHL) playoff game in 2003 that he appeared to briefly lose 20 consciousness as he **temporarily**[1] stayed down on the ice motionless, and then seemed wobbly while being helped off the playing surface. Amazingly, he nevertheless returned to finish the game. It is now clear, however, that he had suffered a concussion, 25 one of six throughout his career. This concussion was apparently so severe that he not only has no memory of the hit, but he has no memory of the game itself. In fact, he does not even remember the next game

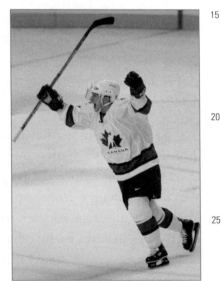

Canadian hockey player Paul Kariya
Image credit: AP/AFLO

he played, which was the seventh and last game of the Stanley Cup finals—the most 30 important game of the season in the NHL.

3 By today's standards, a player hitting another player in the head that hard seems unacceptable, and allowing a player who has suffered such a serious blow to the head to return to the game seems unconscionable. Professional sports fortunately now take the risk of brain injuries quite seriously. For one thing, stricter rules with 35 harsher penalties **deter**[2] players from targeting another player's head. In addition, the implementation of concussion protocols has helped ensure that players who suffer head injuries get appropriate medical care. Concussion protocols vary by sport, but generally speaking, players who suffer a blow to the head are taken out of the game and carefully examined at the game site itself to make sure that they are not showing signs of a head injury. If they are showing signs of a concussion, they are typically removed from a team's lineup for an extended period of time until they have made a full recovery. These changes to the rules thereby help reduce the likelihood of players suffering blows to the head, and help ensure that those who have suffered a concussion do not resume full-contact activities until they have fully recovered.

23 CD

4 Such changes to the rules in contact sports are **crucial**[3] for player safety, especially since recent research has shown that traumatic brain injuries can have severe and lasting consequences. One of the main concerns when it comes to suffering multiple concussions is the risk of developing chronic traumatic encephalopathy (CTE), a condition that is worrisome for several reasons. First, symptoms typically do not appear until several years after suffering traumatic brain injuries, which means that athletes may be deceived by the fact that they recover from each individual

> カリヤ選手が、父
> 方の祖先の母国とつ
> ながりを持つ機会を
> 逃してしまった件に
> ついて、章末の
> Point of Interest を
> 読んでみよう。

concussion. Second, and most importantly, the symptoms of CTE can be devastating, and include behavioral changes, memory loss, and even physical issues like tremors and coordination problems. In short, CTE is an insidious condition that can become debilitating.

24 CD

5 The reality is that it is impossible to completely eliminate the risk of head injuries in contact sports, but recent changes in sports like football and hockey are at least helping reduce the frequency and severity of such injuries. This is obviously a welcome change from a player safety standpoint, given that such injuries can profoundly affect an athlete's regular life. For instance, retired NFL quarterback Brett Favre, who believes he may have suffered many undiagnosed concussions during his Hall of Fame career, stated during a radio interview that he does not remember his daughter playing youth soccer one summer. This is clearly a frightening degree of memory loss, and so if head injuries can cause this, then preventing the kind of hits that lead to head injuries is a worthwhile endeavor. The problem, though, is that hard hitting has been a core feature of sports like football and hockey, and hard hits have long been a staple of the highlight reels for these sports. New rules that soften the hitting therefore make these sports less entertaining for some fans. However, it has been said that the games we play reveal a lot about us, and so if we are to view society today as modern and civilized, then it seems as though this kind of excessive brutality is best left in the past.

Vince Lombardi「ヴィンス・ロンバルディ（1913-70）」　**allegedly**「伝えられるところでは」　**Paul Kariya**「ポール・カリヤ（1974-）」　**wobbly**「ふらふらする」　**concussion**「脳振とう」　**unconscionable**「許しがたい」　**protocol**「治療プログラム」　**chronic traumatic encephalopathy**「慢性外傷性脳症」　**devastating**「壊滅的な」　**tremor**「震え」　**coordination**「協調」　**debilitating**「徐々に深刻化する」　**contact sport**「コンタクトスポーツ（対戦選手との身体の接触が許されているスポーツ）」　**severity**「重さ」　**Brett Favre**「ブレット・ファーヴ（1969-）」　**Hall of Fame**「（栄誉）殿堂」　**staple**「定番」　**reel**「映像」

Vocabulary

Use the context in the reading section to figure out the meaning of each underlined word below.

1. … as he **temporarily** stayed down on the ice …

   a. extensively　　b. painfully　　　c. frighteningly　d. briefly

2. … harsher penalties **deter** players from …

   a. decide　　　b. demand　　　c. discourage　　d. divide

3. … are **crucial** for player safety …

   a. essential　　b. extreme　　c. invalid　　　d. expensive

Comprehension

Read each statement below carefully, and then based on the information presented in this chapter, write "T" if it is true or "F" if it is false.

1. _____ The quote attributed to Vince Lombardi suggests that players should not just focus on winning, but also make sure to enjoy the game.

2. _____ Head injuries used to be more common, but professional sports leagues have implemented new rules to help prevent them.

3. _____ Paul Kariya was hit so hard during a 2003 hockey game that he left the game and even had to miss the next game.

4. _____ When players get hit in the head, they are now checked for CTE at the game site itself before being allowed to get back in the game.

5. _____ According to the author, hard hitting that causes head injuries does not seem to fit with a more humane modern society.

Summary

Listen carefully to the audio recording for this section and fill in the blanks in the paragraph below.

There is a lot of hard-hitting action in popular contact sports like ice hockey and American football, and sometimes big hits can 1)_____ in serious head injuries. The biggest concern when it comes to head injuries is the risk that suffering 2)_____ concussions could lead to chronic traumatic encephalopathy. This is a debilitating 3)_____ with symptoms that arise years after the traumatic injuries occurred. While vicious hits were not all that uncommon in such sports in the past, growing awareness of the 4)_____ of traumatic brain injuries has resulted in concussion protocols and new rules prohibiting hits that target another player's head. Some fans may be unhappy that these sports have taken away some of the hard-hitting of the past, but the 5)_____ to players makes it clear that these changes are long overdue.

Discussion

Write a short response to the question below. Be prepared to discuss your answer out loud with fellow students if your instructor asks you to do so.

Of all the sports shown on television, which one is your favorite to watch? Please explain your answer.

....

....

....

🌐 Point of Interest

In 1998, Paul Kariya was on track to play for Team Canada during the Winter Olympics in Nagano, Japan. His father was Japanese-Canadian, and so this would have given Paul the opportunity to play for his own country's national hockey team, in his father's ancestral homeland. Right before the Olympics were about to start, however, he unfortunately suffered a concussion during an NHL game, which forced him to miss the Olympics.

Fake News

How does false information pass off as news?

2016年の米大統領選挙でトランプ氏が勝利を収めて以来、フェイクニュースが人々の関心を集めている。虚偽情報がニュースとして拡散するとき、選挙結果にどの程度の影響を与えるのだろうか。主要メディアでさえ誤った情報を広めてしまうことがあるのは、なぜだろうか。また、私たちはニュースとどのように付き合うといいのだろうか。

American President Donald Trump and the mainstream press began a famously antagonistic relationship from the moment he took office, with some journalists openly opposing him, and with the president at times calling the mainstream press "fake news."

Image credit: The White House

Getting Started

To help you connect with this chapter's topic, take a moment to think about the questions below, and then write a short sentence to answer each one.

1. How often do you check the news?

   _____

2. What news story do you remember seeing that later turned out to be false?

   _____

3. What is your main source for news?

   _____

Reading

1 The topic of fake news has garnered a lot of attention in the wake of the 2016 American presidential election, in which Donald Trump pulled off one of the most surprising victories in modern political history. Analysts have since been debating

5 how such a seemingly long-shot candidate could have pulled off this **stunning**[1] victory, and one possibility that has gotten a lot of consideration is that fake news stories may have helped sway some undecided voters.

U.S. President Donald Trump
Image credit: The White House

10 Though it is impossible to catalogue every fake news story that circulated before the election, several studies have looked at fake news in the run-up to the election and have concluded that more than half of the fake

15 news stories relating to the election featured information favorable to Trump. Let us therefore take a closer look at the issue of fake news to learn more about how much influence false information passed off as news has on the outcome of elections, and how even mainstream news outlets can make mistakes and spread false information.

20 **2** Fake news can mean a lot of things, but generally speaking, the expression refers to news stories that include fabricated information. In some cases, creators are motivated by profit. For example, in 2016 there were over a hundred fake news sites based out of Macedonia, where the operators were presumably looking to simply generate ad revenue from clickbait headlines. In other cases, campaign operatives and

25 activists spread false information for political gain. Regardless of the source, fake news can get a large audience. One study, for instance, looked at 41 pro-Clinton fake news stories and 115 pro-Trump fake news stories, and the former were shared 7.6 million times, while the latter were shared 30.3 million times on Facebook. Given that these 156 news stories alone were shared an astounding 37.9 million times, and given that

30 there was obviously a lot more fake news circulating shortly before the election, it is clear that fake news can reach a lot of people.

3 With regard to how much influence fake news actually had, it appears that fake news stories likely did not sway very many people in the 2016 presidential election. Several studies have shown that it was actually a relatively small percentage of

35 the population that consumed most of the fake news viewed online. These people were likely already very conservative or very liberal, and if they did believe the pieces of fake news they were consuming, it was likely because the fake news stories fit with their

preexisting political beliefs. This means that fake news stories like, for instance, the Pope endorsing Donald Trump for president in 2016, likely had little influence since only a small subset of those who already supported Trump's candidacy would have accepted this as true without verifying it.

4 False information has also appeared in the mainstream news media. For 5 example, a news story broke in 2017 on a major American news network claiming that Donald Trump had asked someone to make contact with Russian officials during the 2016 presidential election. The news appears to have affected the stock market, given that stock prices dropped briefly afterward as traders likely expected impeachment and the kind of political instability that creates volatility in the economy. Several hours later, however, the story was corrected and

トランプ米大統領の
フェイクニュース賞
について、章末の 10
Point of Interest を
読んでみよう。

instead stated that the request to contact Russian officials was actually made after the election, which is inconsequential and fairly routine for an incoming administration. In another example from 2017, a short clip of President Trump seemingly dumping 15 food recklessly into a koi pond during a trip to Japan went viral and some major news outlets around the world showed the video. The clip is zoomed in on President Trump as he gives the fish a couple of scoops and then suddenly dumps the food from his container. However, the footage turned out to be **grossly**[2] misleading, for it was cut from a longer, zoomed-out video that features a lengthier feeding session with 20 President Trump and Prime Minister Abe. In the unaltered video, they feed the fish at length, and then the Japanese leader tosses the last bit of food from his container, after which the American leader proceeds to do the same.

5 In the end, it is clear that there is a lot of false information that passes off as news. While most fake news stories are likely inconsequential, the rise of "deepfakes" 25 could be a game-changer. American comedian Jordan Peele created a model example of a deepfake by using video footage of Barack Obama that is seamlessly altered so that the former president's lips move perfectly in sync with Peele's verbal **imitation**[3] of Obama saying controversial things. Peele made this video to raise awareness about deepfakes, and it does indeed help show how such videos can look and sound 30 incredibly real. Perhaps more worrisome, however, is the way that big tech companies and some governments are trying to combat fake news. Tech companies like Google and Facebook are under increasing pressure to rein in fake news, which means that a small group of very powerful companies that already have vast control over the flow of information may end up having even more control. It is therefore crucial that people 35 develop the kind of critical thinking skills needed to discern real news from fake news, so that we do not end up having to call on governments and tech companies to determine what people should and should not be allowed to view, which would result in a situation where the cure is worse than the disease.

fake「偽の」 garner「集める」 long-shot「見込みのない」 sway「左右する」 run-up「前段階」 pass off「思い込ませる」 fabricate「捏造（ねつぞう）する」 clickbait「クリック誘導」 operative「工作員」 pro-Clinton「クリントンを支持する」 endorsing「支持する」 impeachment「弾劾」 instability「不安定」 volatility「不安定」 inconsequential「取るに足らない」 incoming「後継の」 clip「映像を短く切り取ったもの」 zoom in「クローズアップで映す」 scoop「ひとすくい」 footage「映像」 zoomed-out「被写体から遠ざかった」 pass off「通る」 deepfake「ディープフェイク（人物画像合成技術を使用して作成された偽の動画）」 game-changer「状況を一変させる契機」 Jordan Peele「ジョーダン・ピール (1979-)」 Barack Obama「バラク・オバマ（1961- ）」 sync「映像と音声の同期」 combat「闘う」 rein「立ち向かう」 discern「見分ける」

Vocabulary

Use the context in the reading section to figure out the meaning of each underlined word below.

1. … pulled off this **stunning** victory …
   - a. paralyzing
   - b. shocking
   - c. interesting
   - d. beautiful
2. … turned out to be **grossly** misleading …
   - a. falsely
   - b. honestly
   - c. significantly
   - d. slightly
3. … verbal **imitation** of Obama saying …
   - a. insult
   - b. praise
   - c. evaluation
   - d. impression

Comprehension

Read each statement below carefully, and then based on the information presented in this chapter, write "T" if it is true or "F" if it is false.

1. _____ There were only 41 pro-Clinton news stories and 115 pro-Trump fake news stories that were circulating before the election.

2. _____ Fake news stories likely did not affect the decisions of voters since those who believe fake news were already very liberal or conservative.

3. _____ The Pope actually endorsed Donald Trump for president in 2016, but most people mistakenly believed that this was fake news.

4. _____ President Trump tossed the remaining food from his container in a koi pond, after which Prime Minister Abe did the same.

5. _____ The author argues that fake news is a serious concern, but having governments and big tech filter the news could be even worse.

Summary

Listen carefully to the audio recording for this section and fill in the blanks in the paragraph below.

There is a lot of information that is passed off as real news when in fact it is 1)_____ fabricated, or the result of serious mistakes by journalists. The issue of fake news has become an important topic of discussion as 2)_____ grow over the possibility of fake news impacting how people vote in elections. Though such concerns are clearly justified, it appears that it is mostly people who already have firmly 3)_____ political views who are most likely to view fake news. While fake news has so far likely not had much 4)_____ on elections, what are known as deepfakes could potentially affect how people vote. If people fail to develop the critical thinking skills needed to 5)_____ between real and fake news, it raises the prospect of big tech companies and governments increasingly telling us what we can and cannot view.

Discussion

Write a short response to the question below. Be prepared to discuss your answer out loud with fellow students if your instructor asks you to do so.

What can you do to verify that the news you read and watch is actually accurate? Please explain your answer.

....

....

....

🌐 Point of Interest

American President Donald Trump released what he called the "Fake News Awards" on January 17, 2018. It was essentially a list featuring eleven entries, most of which were actual news stories about him that had notable errors or distortions at the time of publication.

Dead as a Dodo

Why are so many species facing extinction?

現在、地球には 800 万以上の動植物が生息しているが、そのうち 100 万種は絶滅の危機に瀕していると言われている。その最大の理由は、ある種（しゅ）の優位性によるものだという。その種とはホモ・サピエンス、つまり私たち人類だ。人間の活動が、多くの動植物の生態を脅かしている現状について考えよう。

The American bison was nearly completely wiped out by the end of the nineteenth century. Conservation efforts have fortunately helped restore this iconic North American species, and its population is now stable.

Image credit: The author

Getting Started

To help you connect with this chapter's topic, take a moment to think about the questions below, and then write a short sentence to answer each one.

1. What wildlife have you ever seen first-hand in nature?

   _____

2. What wild animal would you most like to encounter in nature?

   _____

3. How many different plant and animal species do you think there are today?

   _____

Reading

1 Our planet is teeming with life. A recent study drove this point home by revealing that approximately 7.77 million animal species and 298,000 plant species currently live on Earth. All living things today are the result of an evolutionary process whereby some organisms developed traits that helped them pass on their genes, while those that lacked the traits needed to survive in a given environment died off. Though 5 it is true that extinction has claimed countless species over the course of our planet's history, the threat of extinction today may be more pronounced than ever before for many species, due to the dominance of one species in particular: Homo sapiens. Though the name of our species is Latin for "wise man," humanity as a whole has not yet shown much wisdom with regard to managing the natural environment, and as we 10 will see in this chapter, the threat of extinction is growing rapidly.

2 The Intergovernmental Science-Policy Platform on Biodiversity and Ecosystem Services (IPBES) released the results of a study on biodiversity in 2019, and the findings from this study are quite troubling. Out of the approximately eight million plant and animal species on Earth today, about a million species face the threat of 15 extinction, and many of them face this threat "within decades." One of the major reasons for this is that humans have significantly **altered**[1] about two thirds of the world's marine environments and three fourths of our planet's land. Humans are using almost three quarters of freshwater sources and over a third of the land on Earth to produce crops or raise livestock. With so much land and so many water-based areas 20 having already been dramatically altered by humans, more and more species will end up with relatively little living space as human activities alter even more of the natural environment, meaning that many species will indeed end up facing the very real threat of extinction in the wild.

3 In some cases, poaching is the biggest menace to certain species. Tiger bones 25 and skins, for example, are valuable commodities, which has made tigers valuable targets for poachers. Rhinoceros horns are even more valuable, and as a result, poachers are quickly driving rhinos to the edge of extinction. For many species, however, it is not poaching that threatens their existence, but rather, as shown by the IPBES study, ordinary human activities. Climate change, for 30

> 密猟に対抗するための国際協定について、章末の Point of Interest を読んでみよう。

instance, may be inextricably connected to the welfare of many different species. The effects of climate change could end up changing some habitats so significantly that certain species may not be able to survive. In conjunction with the development of land for housing and agricultural purposes, it is obvious that human activities truly 35 have the potential to easily wipe out entire species.

4 One of the most notable sources for data on which species are endangered is the Red List of Threatened Species, created by the International Union for Conservation of Nature (IUCN). There are several categories for species that are to some degree currently at risk of going extinct, including "Vulnerable," "Endangered," and "Critically Endangered." For example, polar bears are listed as vulnerable, while red pandas are listed as endangered, and the Javan rhinoceros is listed as critically endangered. A study titled *The Great Elephant Census* serves as a good **warning**[2] for how quickly a species can

A red panda on the move
Image credit: The author

experience a rapid drop in population and possibly end up threatened or endangered. This study found that the African elephant population dropped by thirty percent in the span of just seven years. Even more troubling, the study found that the rate of population decline is eight percent per year, and this annual rate is accelerating. In 2014, the last year of this massive study, the African elephant population was down to 352,271, and while this seems like a large population, the current rate of decline will likely result in the African elephant becoming an endangered species.

5 Though many governments around the world have environmental laws and wildlife preserves that **protect**[3] various species, such measures appear to be insufficient in the face of growing pressure on the environment. With the global population expected to hit eight billion sometime in the first half of the 2020s, and then approach ten billion around 2050, it is very likely that the threat of extinction for many species around the world will grow even more severe. It seems, then, that the most important step for helping protect endangered species is to find ways to limit human population growth, and to find more efficient ways to sustain human beings so that we do not continue to encroach on wildlife habitats. Given that extinction is irreversible, the loss of an entire species is unlike many of the other typical mistakes that we can simply correct later on. The issue of endangered species is therefore an especially urgent one, and so it is critical that we start living up to the "sapiens" part of Homo sapiens and find real solutions to this problem before it is too late.

NOTES ···

teeming「たくさんいる」 extinction「絶滅」 **Intergovernmental Science-Policy Platform on Biodiversity and Ecosystem Services**「生物多様性及び生態系サービスに関する政府間科学 - 政策プラットフォーム」 livestock「家畜類」 **Red List of Threatened Species**「絶滅危惧種リスト」 **International Union for Conservation of Nature**「国際自然保護連合」 Vulnerable「危急」 Endangered「絶滅危機」 **Critically Endangered**「絶滅寸前」 Javan rhinoceros「ジャワサイ」 census「全数」 population「生息数」

poaching「密漁」 rhino (= rhinoceros)「サイ」 inextricably「密接に」 habitat「生息地」 wipe out「絶滅させる」 preserve「保護区」 encroach「侵害する」 sapiens「現人類の」

Vocabulary

Use the context in the reading section to figure out the meaning of each underlined word below.

1. … have significantly **altered** about two thirds …
   - a. changed
   - b. renovated
   - c. fixed
   - d. damaged
2. … a good **warning** for how quickly a species can …
   - a. caution
   - b. calculation
   - c. communication
   - d. threat
3. … for helping **protect** endangered species …
   - a. trust
   - b. determine
   - c. safeguard
   - d. excite

Comprehension

Read each statement below carefully, and then based on the information presented in this chapter, write "T" if it is true or "F" if it is false.

1. _____ According to the results of the IPBES study released in 2019, approximately eight million species face the threat of extinction.

2. _____ About two thirds of aquatic environments and three fourths of the planet's land have been significantly altered by human activities.

3. _____ There are only a few polar bears left in the wild, and so the IUCN has listed this species as critically endangered.

4. _____ Poaching is a serious threat to rhinos, which are valued for their skin and their bones.

5. _____ The author suggests that reducing population growth for humans could be an effective way to help protect endangered species.

Summary

Listen carefully to the audio recording for this section and fill in the blanks in the paragraph below.

There are approximately over eight million plant and animal species on Earth today, and according to a 1)_____ study, a million of these species may soon face the threat of extinction. While species throughout history have gone extinct for 2)_____ reasons, human activities are currently the most significant threat for most species. For example, unique animals like tigers and rhinos are often 3)_____ by poachers, who are perhaps the biggest threat to such species. The most common way that human activities 4)_____ most species, however, is by using land for settlement and agriculture, which leads to the destruction of natural habitats. Given that the human population is growing rapidly, it appears that the threat to many species will only get 5)_____, and so it is vital that we strive to improve conservation efforts.

Discussion

Write a short response to the question below. Be prepared to discuss your answer out loud with fellow students if your instructor asks you to do so.

What endangered species do you worry about most in terms of it possibly going extinct? Please explain your answer.

....

....

....

🌐 Point of Interest

The Convention on International Trade in Endangered Species of Wild Fauna and Flora (CITES) is one way that has been developed to help deal with poaching, by establishing stringent regulations for the flow of products derived from endangered species across borders. CITES first went into force in 1975, and there are now 183 countries that have agreed to join this convention.

It's a Dry Heat

Where is the hottest place on Earth?

日本の最高気温は、2018年7月に埼玉県熊谷市で観測された41.1度であるが、世界最高気温の記録について聞いたことがあるだろうか。それは米国カリフォルニア州にあるデスヴァレーで、最高気温は56.7度、また1カ月の平均最高気温が42度弱の記録も残っている。この地が地球上で一番暑い場所なのはなぜだろう。

Death Valley features scorching summer temperatures, including the highest surface air temperature ever recorded on Earth. Dante's View serves as one of the best spots to see this American national park's layout.

Image credit: The author

Getting Started

To help you connect with this chapter's topic, take a moment to think about the questions below, and then write a short sentence to answer each one.

1. What is the hottest outdoor temperature you have ever experienced?

   _____

2. Would you rather have hot and humid weather, or hot and dry weather?

   _____

3. Which do you prefer: winter weather or summer weather?

   _____

Reading

1 Many places throughout the world get periods of extreme heat at one time or another. For example, the city of Kumagaya recorded a temperature of just over forty-one degrees Celsius in July of 2018, which set the record for the highest temperature ever recorded in Japan. This is obviously pretty hot, but many places experience even
5 higher temperatures, and in some places the temperature can actually reach well over fifty degrees Celsius. While many locations around the world see some pretty high temperatures, there is only one spot that can rightly be called the hottest place on Earth: Death Valley. Let us take a closer look at this seemingly unwelcoming place to find out why it is considered the hottest place on Earth, and why temperatures there
10 can **soar**[1] so high.

2 Death Valley, California, is part of the desert landscape that is found throughout much of the American Southwest. It features an average high temperature in July and August of around forty-six degrees Celsius, but temperatures are often significantly higher than this. Most
15 notably, it set the record in 1913 for the hottest surface air temperature ever recorded on Earth: a blistering 56.7 degrees Celsius. The second highest surface air temperature ever

> デスヴァレー（死の谷）という地名の由来について、章末のPoint of Interest を読んでみよう。

recorded is a scorching fifty-four degrees Celsius, and it was also recorded in Death Valley, in June of 2013, though it is worth noting that Mitribah, Kuwait, later recorded
20 this same temperature in July of 2016. In 1972, Death Valley's ground temperature once hit close to ninety-four degrees Celsius, which means that the ground was literally almost hot enough to boil water. Most recently, in July of 2017, Death Valley broke the record for the highest average temperature for a single month, with an average temperature of nearly forty-two degrees Celsius.

25 **3** Death Valley is not only exceptionally hot, it is also extremely dry. In fact, calling this place dry is an understatement. There are two years, 1929 and 1953, when there was absolutely no rain on record, and over the course of forty months spanning from 1931 to 1934, Death Valley received less than two centimeters of rain, and on average there is less than five centimeters of annual rainfall. While hot and dry
30 makes survival difficult, at least it is more comfortable than hot and humid. People who **reside**[2] in the American Southwest, in places like Las Vegas and Phoenix, thus often say: "at least it's a dry heat." The National Weather Service in the United States uses what is called the Heat Index to include the effects of humidity on perceived temperature. For example, if relative humidity is fifteen percent, then forty-six degrees
35 Celsius will simply feel like forty-six degrees Celsius. If relative humidity increases to twenty percent, however, forty-six degrees Celsius will actually feel like just over forty-

nine degrees Celsius, and if relative humidity rises to thirty percent, it will feel like nearly fifty-seven degrees Celsius.

4 According to the National Park Service, which cares for American national parks like Death Valley, a couple of reasons explain why Death Valley is so hot and so arid. For one thing, winter storms come in from the Pacific Ocean, but several mountain ranges lie between the coast and Death Valley. The clouds therefore have to rise up to cross these mountain ranges, at which point they begin to cool off as they reach higher altitudes, which causes them to lose their moisture in the form of rain. By the time they cross over to the eastern side of the mountains, where Death Valley is located, these clouds have very little moisture left, and so they seldom bring rain. As for Death Valley's incredible heat, it is largely due to its long and narrow shape, and due to its depth of eighty-six meters below sea level, which is the lowest elevation in North America. Moreover, with so little vegetation in the region, sunlight easily heats up the surface, and then the heat radiates out of the ground and rocks, while the surrounding mountains help trap the heat in Death Valley's depths.

5 Despite its name, Death Valley is not as lifeless as might be expected—though it is certainly not a place for those with a weak constitution. The animals that inhabit Death Valley, and much of the American Southwest in general, are tough and fierce survivors. Rattlesnakes, scorpions, and various spiders, for example, are fearsome hunters in tight spaces, while coyotes **wander**[3] the land and scavenge on whatever they can find or kill. Vegetation is sparse, and only rugged plant life like cacti and yuccas, and certain wildflowers, can endure Death Valley's punishing climate. Though very few people would want to live in Death Valley, many do enjoy visiting this seemingly inhospitable national park, which is only about a four-hour drive away from Los Angeles and only about a two-hour drive away

A coyote searching for food
Image credit: The author

from Las Vegas. For most people, then, Death Valley serves as a quintessential example for one of the most classic expressions in the English language: "nice place to visit, but wouldn't want to live there."

NOTES

Celsius「セ氏」 **blistering**「焼け付くような」 **scorching**「灼熱の」 **understatement**「控えめな表現」 **National Weather Service**「(米) 国立気象局」 **arid**「乾燥した」 **vegetation**「植物」 **radiate**「広がる」 **rattlesnake**「ガラガラヘビ」 **scorpion**「サソリ」 **scavenge**「あさる」 **cacti**「サボテン (cactus の複数形)」 **yucca**「ユカ」 **inhospitable**「住むのに適さない」 **quintessential**「典型的な」

Vocabulary

Use the context in the reading section to figure out the meaning of each underlined word below.

1. … why temperatures there can **soar** so …

        a. motivate   b. increase   c. fly   d. tumble

2. … who **reside** in the American Southwest …

        a. appreciate   b. examine   c. inhabit   d. fluctuate

3. … coyotes **wander** the land …

        a. damage   b. roam   c. leave   d. arrive

Comprehension

Read each statement below carefully, and then based on the information presented in this chapter, write "T" if it is true or "F" if it is false.

1. _____ The highest temperature ever recorded is 56.7 degrees Celsius, which was in Death Valley in 2016.

2. _____ The fact that Death Valley is so dry makes its extremely hot temperatures feel even hotter.

3. _____ Over the course of forty months from 1931 to 1934 there was absolutely no rain on record in Death Valley.

4. _____ One reason that explains why Death Valley is so hot and dry is its low elevation.

5. _____ According to the author, Death Valley is quite inhospitable and so it does not make for a very good place to visit.

Summary

Listen carefully to the audio recording for this section and fill in the blanks in the paragraph below.

Many spots around the world experience extreme heat, but Death Valley in the United States 1)_____ out as the hottest place on Earth. It holds many records, including the highest temperature ever 2)_____, just under fifty-seven degrees Celsius in 1913, and the highest average temperature for a month, nearly forty-two degrees Celsius in July of 2017. Death Valley is also 3)_____ dry, and there are actually two years when there was no rain whatsoever on record. Death Valley's geographical features account for its 4)_____ climate, for its shape, depth, and proximity to tall mountains all help create the perfect conditions for an intensely hot and dry climate. As forbidding as this place seems, Death Valley is 5)_____ a popular tourist destination that is only a few hours away by car from major cities like Los Angeles and Las Vegas.

Discussion

Write a short response to the question below. Be prepared to discuss your answer out loud with fellow students if your instructor asks you to do so.

What is the hottest temperature you have ever experienced? Please explain how difficult it was for you to do things when it was that hot.

....

....

....

⊕ Point of Interest

A group of pioneers heading to California in 1849 tried to avoid crossing the mountains blocking their way by taking a trail that went around them instead. They got lost, wandered through the desert for a couple of months, and ended up stuck in what is now called Death Valley. Some pioneers left on their own, but others stayed and waited for help. Once rescued, one of the pioneers allegedly said on the way out, "good bye, Death Valley," and the name stuck.

Man's Best Friend

Why is the French bulldog a controversial breed?

フレンチブルドッグはフランスのネズミ捕り用犬とイングリッシュ・ブルドッグを掛け合わせた犬種で、その特徴であるつぶれた鼻とコウモリ耳と呼ばれる立ち耳、それに感情のこもった目で人気を集めている。その一方で、フレンチブルドッグは健康上の問題も抱えており、その繁殖について議論を呼ぶ犬種でもある。何が問題視されているのか、見てみよう。

The French bulldog is one of the most photogenic dog breeds, and its bat ears, flat snout, and large soulful eyes generate a wide range of facial expressions. Some appear to have a big wide smile, whereas others, like the one here, appear to have an intensely serious gaze.

Image credit: The author

Getting Started

To help you connect with this chapter's topic, take a moment to think about the questions below, and then write a short sentence to answer each one.

1. How would you describe the French bulldog in this photo?

   _____

2. What kind of pets do you have or have you had in the past?

   _____

3. What is your favorite kind of dog?

   _____

Reading

1 The French bulldog was originally bred in the nineteenth century in France, where it is called the "bouledogue français." However, it is actually half English, since it is the result of breeding French rat-catching dogs with English bulldogs. Though it has clearly retained certain traits from the larger English bulldog, like its muscular frame and flat snout, the French bulldog's so-called "bat ears," along with its pensive 5 and soulful eyes, give it a truly distinctive look. The French bulldog is undeniably charming and photogenic, but numerous health problems belie its charming physical traits. These health problems have actually **generated**[1] some controversy when it comes to breeding French bulldogs, as we will see in this chapter.

2 The French bulldog is rapidly becoming one of the most popular dog 10 breeds. In the United States, for example, it has steadily gone up in the American Kennel Club rankings for most popular dog breeds, from eleventh in 2013 to fourth in 2018. These relatively small dogs have a stocky build, muscular front shoulders, and a thick neck that can make them look quite imposing despite being relatively small in stature. For people who ordinarily do not like small dogs, but live in big cities 15 where smaller housing options often make owning a large dog impractical, the French bulldog is thus an ideal choice. This might explain why the French bulldog recently ranked as the most popular dog breed in cities like Los Angeles, New York City, and San Francisco.

3 Their behavioral traits also add to their appeal. The American Kennel Club 20 describes the French bulldog's temperament as "adaptable, playful, smart." French bulldog owners would likely agree with this assessment, and perhaps add traits like stubborn and feisty. What often gets the most attention, however, is this breed's unique facial expressions, which may be characterized as proud sternness 25 with a touch of clownish joviality. On the one hand, their wrinkled faces and short snouts make these dogs seem very serious and pensive when they sit and quietly **gaze**[2] at their

> フレンチブルドッグの知名度が上がるのに貢献した有名人やメディアとその功罪について、章末のPoint of Interest を読んでみよう。

surroundings. On the other hand, when these dogs get excited and begin to pant hard, their mouths typically curl on the sides to give the appearance of a big smile, which 30 can look a bit comical when combined with their pointy "bat ears."

4 Despite being such a charming breed, the French bulldog is not without controversy. When it comes to controversial dogs, breeds with a reputation for aggression, like the American pit bull terrier, typically come to mind. While it is true that any dog, no matter what breed, can become aggressive if not raised properly, 35 the greatest level of hostility a French bulldog will typically show toward humans is a stern, disapproving look. The reason for controversy surrounding the French bulldog therefore obviously has nothing to do with its temperament, but rather, with the fact that it is brachycephalic, which simply means that it has a short snout. Other brachycephalic breeds include English bulldogs, pugs, boxers, Boston terriers, and bull mastiffs. Though their flat faces are central to their appeal, short snouts can unfortunately leave these dogs susceptible to serious health problems, like brachycephalic airway syndrome. Dogs suffering from this syndrome cannot breathe well, and so when they are exposed to above average temperatures or engage in even just a moderate level of exercise, they can experience life-threatening respiratory distress. This is the reason why, for

Side view of this breed's short snout
Image credit: The author

example, many airlines do not allow brachycephalic breeds to travel in a plane's cargo hold, where the stress of travel and potentially above average temperatures can prove fatal. Out of all brachycephalic breeds, French bulldogs are actually among the most likely to experience extreme symptoms of brachycephalic airway syndrome. Some people therefore argue that it is cruel to breed these dogs, since they are bred to have physically appealing traits that actually act as disabilities.

48

5 Ultimately, there is good reason to argue that the French bulldog could benefit from being bred differently in order to **modify**[3] some of its more troublesome traits. On the other hand, the French bulldog's health challenges are far from insurmountable. Owners simply need to understand the additional challenges that come with this particular breed, such as, more frequent visits to a veterinarian, the need to be especially attentive to climate control in the home, and the need to carefully monitor these dogs when going on any lengthy outdoors excursion. This means that even though this breed's health issues are obviously a great concern, French bulldogs can easily live a full and fruitful life as long as owners remember to take care of these special needs. The bottom line is that the French bulldog's complex personality and quirky physical traits are so charming that owners willingly put up with the added responsibility that comes with owning this type of dog. Given how charming and popular this breed is, then, it seems safe to say that the controversy surrounding these dogs is likely not enough to dampen its popularity with French bulldog enthusiasts, and so this breed's standards will likely not change anytime soon.

snout「鼻」 pensive「物思いに沈んだ」 soulful「感情のこもった」 photogenic「写真写りのよい」 belie「誤った印象を与える」 dog breed「犬種」 stocky「がっしりとした」 imposing「堂々とした」 playful「よくじゃれる」 stubborn「強情そうな」 feisty「気骨のある」 sternness「厳格さ」 joviality「快活」 pant「あえぐ」 pointy「先のとがった」 bat ear「コウモリ耳」 pit bull「ピットブル」闘犬用小型犬 brachycephalic「短頭の」 pug「パグ（短毛・短胴の小型犬）」 bull mastiff「ブルマスチフ（大型の番犬）」 brachycephalic airway syndrome「短頭種気道閉塞症候群」 respiratory「呼吸器の」 cargo hold「貨物室」 disability「身体障害」 bottom line「要点」 quirky「一種独特の」

Vocabulary

Use the context in the reading section to figure out the meaning of each underlined word below.

1. … have actually **generated** some controversy …

        a. caused   b. decided   c. motivated   d. formulated

2. … sit and quietly **gaze** at their …

        a. approach   b. debate   c. wonder   d. stare

3. … in order to **modify** some of its …

        a. create   b. visualize   c. change   d. maintain

Comprehension

Read each statement below carefully, and then based on the information presented in this chapter, write "T" if it is true or "F" if it is false.

1. _____ The French bulldog's popularity has been decreasing in the United States due to this breed's health problems.

2. _____ The American Kennel Club describes this breed's personality as stubborn, playful, and smart.

3. _____ The reason for controversy with French bulldogs is that they are prone to being aggressive and they often have breathing difficulties.

4. _____ English bulldogs, pugs, boxers, Boston terriers, and bull mastiffs are all examples of brachycephalic breeds.

5. _____ The author argues that the French bulldog breed is not likely going to change anytime soon.

Summary

Listen carefully to the audio recording for this section and fill in the blanks in the paragraph below.

French bulldogs are the product of French rat-catching dogs being bred with English bulldogs, and as a 1)_____, this breed has a unique and distinctive look. They are famous for their 2)_____, which comes from their soulful eyes and what are often called "bat ears," and this has helped them become one of the most popular breeds. French bulldogs are unfortunately prone to health problems, largely due to their 3)_____ short snout, which can result in a condition known as brachycephalic airway syndrome. French bulldogs and other short-snout breeds that are 4)_____ to this condition can easily experience breathing difficulties from even just a moderate level of exercise. Though French bulldogs are 5)_____ delicate dogs, they can easily lead a full life if owners are careful to attend to their special needs.

Discussion

Write a short response to the question below. Be prepared to discuss your answer out loud with fellow students if your instructor asks you to do so.

It is often said that everyone is either a dog person or a cat person. Which would you pick to describe yourself? Please explain.

....

....

....

🌐 Point of Interest

A number of celebrities apparently have or have had a French bulldog, most notably Dwayne Johnson (also known as "The Rock"), Hugh Jackman, and Lady Gaga. French bulldogs have also appeared in movies like *Due Date*, starring Robert Downey Jr., and are frequently featured in advertising. This kind of exposure has undoubtedly helped increase the popularity of French bulldogs, but some people may end up getting this kind of dog purely due to its photogenic qualities, without realizing just how much special care these dogs need, which can end up being bad for both dogs and owners alike.

The Wild West

Why is the city of Phoenix growing so quickly?

「太陽の谷」と呼ばれることも多いアリゾナ州のフェニックス大都市圏は、米国の中でも急速に発展している地域である。フェニックス周辺が、比喩的にも文字通りの意味でも、最もホットで魅力的な地であるのはなぜだろうか。

The saguaro cactus, which is perhaps the most famous feature of the Sonoran Desert, is prevalent throughout the Phoenix Metropolitan Area. These tree-like cacti can go over twelve meters in height and can live for up to two hundred years.

Image credit: The author

Getting Started

To help you connect with this chapter's topic, take a moment to think about the questions below, and then write a short sentence to answer each one.

1. Which large American metropolitan area do you most want to visit?

   _____

2. How big is the population of your hometown?

   _____

3. How is the size of the population in your hometown changing?

   _____

Reading

1 Arizona cities in the late nineteenth century were known for their Wild West atmosphere, with one of the best examples of this Wild West atmosphere being the legendary 1881 gunfight at the O.K. Corral in the city of Tombstone. Today, however, Arizona cities have come a long way since their early Wild

5　West days, and this is especially true for the Phoenix Metropolitan Area. According to 2018 statistics, nearly five million people now live in the Phoenix Metropolitan Area, and it is the second fastest growing metropolitan area in the United States. Most of this metro area is **situated**[1] in Maricopa

アリゾナ州が、開拓時代の西部地方のどのような名残りを今もとどめているのか、章末の Point of Interest を読んでみよう。

10　County, which is the fastest growing county in the country. It is therefore clear that the Phoenix area truly is a hot destination, literally and figuratively, so let us take a closer look to see what makes this part of the United States such an attractive destination.

2 The Phoenix Metropolitan Area, often colloquially referred to as the Valley of the Sun, includes Phoenix, which is the state capital, and many smaller cities around

15　it, most notably Scottsdale, Glendale, Mesa, and Tempe. The area is surrounded by a vast desert environment, and much of the architecture and urban layout has focused on blending into and incorporating the beauty of the surrounding natural landscape. Many buildings outside

20　of the downtown area are only a few stories high, and so the iconic Camelback Mountain that stands tall in the heart of the Phoenix area and the various other desert mountains

25　that encircle it can all be viewed easily from many places throughout the Valley. These mountains all offer numerous hiking trails that make it

Downtown Phoenix and Camelback Mountain
Image credit: The author

possible for people to enjoy the local environment first-hand. Several locations in the

30　city of Scottsdale, for example, feature a large network of trails that run through the McDowell Sonoran Preserve. These trails give hikers a chance to observe the Sonoran Desert's unique variety of plant life, like the **majestic**[2] saguaro cactus and the hazardous jumping cholla, pieces of which can easily attach to people if even just barely touched. Hikers occasionally also get to see wildlife, like coyotes and various lizards.

3 The Phoenix area is also known for sports, and it is one of the relatively

35　few metropolitan areas in the United States with a team in all four major American professional sports leagues: the Arizona Diamondbacks for Major League Baseball (MLB), the Arizona Cardinals for the National Football League (NFL), the Phoenix Suns for the National Basketball Association (NBA), and the Arizona Coyotes for the National Hockey League (NHL). In addition, the city of Tempe is home to Arizona State University (ASU). Though ASU was ranked first in the 2018 *U.S. News and World Report* university rankings for the "most innovative schools" category, it is also known for its collegiate sports programs, particularly its football and basketball teams. The university's teams play in the Pac-12 conference, which is one of the strongest conferences in the National Collegiate Athletic Association (NCAA), and its football and basketball games always draw large crowds. The Phoenix area also features an abundance of top-tier golf courses, public parks and natural-grass fields for recreational sports leagues, and even a few man-made lakes for boating and other water sports.

4 Part of the Phoenix area's appeal also relates to what the state of Arizona overall has to offer. Arizona is known as the "Grand Canyon State," and it takes only about four hours by car from Phoenix to get to the state's famous natural wonder. Near the Grand Canyon are two other impressive natural wonders: Monument Valley, which features towering buttes spaced out on relatively flat rocky landscape, and Horseshoe Bend, which features an awe-inspiring pillar-like rocky formation carved out by the Colorado River. Only a two-hour drive from Phoenix is the city of Sedona, which features some **spectacular**[3] scenery like Cathedral Rock and Havasu Falls. Phoenix is also only about two hours away from the city of Flagstaff, which is in the Coconino National Forest area. This area features an abundance of ponderosa pine trees and snow-capped mountains, and is much cooler, which stands in stark contrast to the Phoenix area's desert environment.

5 In the end, it is clear that despite the Phoenix Metropolitan Area's scorching summer temperatures, it is a great place for recreation and outdoor life. Several practical considerations, though, also contribute to its appeal, like the growing job market, and the cost of buying a home, which is typically lower than in other big cities like Los Angeles, New York, and San Francisco. Much of the infrastructure is also relatively new, and so the roads are smooth, the highways are efficiently designed, and many buildings look modern. Finally, people have also been drawn to the Phoenix area due to the fact that it is far less crowded than many of the other major metropolitan areas in the United States. With regard to this last feature, however, it likely will not remain as one of the Phoenix area's selling points much longer, for with no signs of slowing down, the rapid population growth it has been experiencing will increasingly bring its population density in line with other major American metro areas. It therefore appears that this desert oasis that was once part of the Wild West is rapidly becoming a major metropolis that could soon rival some of the most notable metro areas in the United States.

Vocabulary

Use the context in the reading section to figure out the meaning of each underlined word below.

1. … this metro area is **situated** in …
   - a. created
   - b. imagined
   - c. removed
   - d. located

2. … like the **majestic** saguaro cactus …
   - a. glorious
   - b. strange
   - c. confusing
   - d. common

3. … features some **spectacular** scenery …
   - a. regular
   - b. visual
   - c. unreal
   - d. magnificent

Comprehension

Read each statement below carefully, and then based on the information presented in this chapter, write "T" if it is true or "F" if it is false.

1. _____ The Phoenix Metropolitan Area is the second fastest growing metropolitan area in the United States.

2. _____ The city of Scottsdale has a network of trails that allow visitors to experience the Sonoran Desert.

3. _____ The Phoenix area is just one of relatively few metro areas in the United States with three professional sports teams.

4. _____ Arizona is known as the Grand Canyon State, and this canyon is only about a four-hour drive from Phoenix.

5. _____ The author concludes that due to the Phoenix area's new infrastructure it won't get crowded as the population grows.

① 55

Summary

Listen carefully to the audio recording for this section and fill in the blanks in the paragraph below.

The Phoenix Metropolitan Area, which is often called the Valley of the Sun, is one of the fastest 1)_____ metropolitan areas in the United States. Many reasons can account for why so many people are moving to this metro area, and some of the main ones may be the 2)_____ beautiful landscape and relatively new infrastructure. The Phoenix metro area is also famous for its sports 3)_____, highlighted by the fact that it has a professional team in all four major sports leagues in the United States. The state of Arizona more broadly may also contribute to the area's appeal, for there are a 4)_____ of great natural wonders within driving range. Whatever the reason why people are moving there, it is clear that the Phoenix area is growing 5)_____, and it may soon become a bit more crowded like other major American metropolitan areas.

Discussion

Write a short response to the question below. Be prepared to discuss your answer out loud with fellow students if your instructor asks you to do so.

Would you prefer to live in a large metropolitan area with millions of residents, or to live in a small town. Please explain your answer.

....

....

....

🌐 Point of Interest

Arizona still retains one notable trait from its Wild West days: residents are legally allowed to carry firearms, either visibly or concealed, and do not require any kind of permit or license to do so. There are certain age restrictions, and some places like sports venues and some commercial establishments prohibit firearms on their premises. Unlike the old Wild West days, however, discharging a firearm in public is a serious offense, and law enforcement takes any kind of gun crime very seriously.

Man versus Beast

How much of a threat do bears pose to people?

北米ではクマは自然の景観にしっかり溶け込んだ存在となっているが、人間の命を奪うことができるだけに恐ろしい存在と思うことがあっても無理はない。人がクマに襲われると大々的に報道される傾向があるため、クマは凶暴で人間にとって危険だと考えられがちであるが、果たしてどれほどの脅威なのだろうか。他の動物とも比較して考えてみよう。

Black bears, such as the ones pictured here, roam throughout most of Canada and the United States. Though they generally do not pose a threat to humans, situations do occasionally arise that lead them to attack people.

Image credit: The author

Getting Started

To help you connect with this chapter's topic, take a moment to think about the questions below, and then write a short sentence to answer each one.

1. Which animal do you think is the deadliest for humans?

   _____

2. What is the most dangerous animal you have seen in person?

   _____

3. What is the scariest movie you have seen that depicts an animal attack?

   _____

Reading

1 Bears are arguably North America's most majestic creatures, and they instill in most people a sense of awe. They also instill in some people a sense of fear, and so when one does attack a human, the incident tends to get highly publicized, especially when the attack is fatal. Such attacks can create the **perception**[1] that bears are vicious animals that represent a serious threat to people. However, despite the fact that human 5 settlements are often in close proximity to these powerful animals, bear attacks are relatively rare, and these creatures are actually far more likely to avoid humans than attack them. Let us therefore take a closer look at bear attacks in North America, and then compare them with fatal animal attacks on humans by different animal species to find out just how much of a threat bears really are to humans. 10

2 The threat of a bear attack is a serious concern for anyone who is alone in the North American wilderness, where black bears roam throughout much of the United States and Canada, and where brown bears roam much of the northwestern part of the continent. It is relatively rare to encounter bears, since they typically avoid humans, 15 but people can easily find themselves in mortal danger in those rare instances when they come face to face with a bear, since attacks by these powerful animals often result in gruesome injuries that can 20 prove fatal. That being said, fatal attacks are exceptionally rare given that hundreds of thousands of bears roam the North American landscape, often within range of

North American brown bear
Image credit: The author

cities and parks frequented by people. An analysis of bear attacks from 2000 to 2017 25 in the United States and Canada reveals just how rare fatal attacks really are, for there were forty-six fatal bear attacks during this time frame, and of these, twenty-five were by black bears and twenty-one by brown bears, for an average of a little less than three per year. Although these attacks are occasionally unprovoked, in many cases humans inadvertently provoke bear attacks by hiking in areas where mothers are foraging with 30 their cubs, for instance, or by leaving open food containers in camping areas.

3 In the **sparsely**[2] populated northernmost parts of North America, namely Alaska and northern Canada, another type of bear roams free: the polar bear. Polar bears rely on seasonal sea ice to hunt, but the changing climate is forcing polar bears to stay ashore longer. This results in polar bears being increasingly drawn to human 35 settlements for food, which raises the risk of polar bear attacks. For instance, in the small town of Arviat, which lies along the Hudson Bay coastline and is in the Canadian territory of Nunavut, even the Halloween event of trick-or-treating had to be canceled in 2014 and 2015 due to the presence of polar bears, before resuming in 2016 when volunteers helped secure the town for the event. In the summer of 2018, however, things took a turn for the worse when two men were killed in separate polar bear attacks in Nunavut. Polar bears have historically seldom killed humans, and so only time will tell if these are isolated incidents, or if increased contact with humans will indeed make polar bear attacks increasingly common.

59 CD

4 There is no denying that bears can be absolutely **ferocious**[3] animals, but in terms of attacks on humans, they are not as deadly as some of the other top predators around the world. In India and Bangladesh, for example, tigers kill dozens of humans every year. In Tanzania, according to one study, lions killed over five hundred humans over a fifteen-year span beginning in 1990. To really put things in perspective, however, a human getting killed by a bear is rarer than

注目されることも多いサメによる攻撃について、章末のPoint of Interestを読んでみよう。

something considered to be among the rarest of events: getting struck by lightning. According to the National Weather Service in the United States, lightning strikes over the course of a ten-year span, from 2009 to 2018, caused an average of twenty-seven fatalities per year in the United States alone. As such, it is literally far more likely, from a statistical standpoint, to get struck by lightning than killed by a bear in North America.

60 CD

5 In the end, we can say that attacks by bears are undoubtedly terrifying, but they are clearly quite rare in countries like Canada and the United States. Attacks by powerful predators in the developing world are a bit more common, but still pretty rare in comparison with some animals that are actually far less imposing. For instance, the World Health Organization (WHO) estimates that poisonous snakes kill at least eighty thousand people a year, primarily in Asia and Africa. Though snakes are undeniably horrifically lethal for humans, there is one particularly inconspicuous animal that is even deadlier: the mosquito. The WHO estimates that diseases transmitted by mosquitos kill approximately seven hundred thousand people annually, making it the deadliest animal of all for humans. This means that while there is no denying that bears can pose a very real threat to humans in those rare instances when they come in close proximity to people, they are statistically not nearly as dangerous as a wide variety of other animals. The reality is that it is usually possible to avoid situations that make attacks possible in the first place by simply keeping in mind when visiting the North American wilderness that it is bears, not humans, that rule in the wild.

....

Vocabulary

Use the context in the reading section to figure out the meaning of each underlined word below.

1. … can create the **perception** that …
   - a. intuition
   - b. belief
   - c. suspicion
   - d. disappointment

2. … the **sparsely** populated northernmost parts of …
   - a. minimally
   - b. heavily
   - c. unusually
   - d. truly

3. … bears can be absolutely **ferocious** animals …
   - a. beautiful
   - b. savage
   - c. faithful
   - d. deceitful

Comprehension

Read each statement below carefully, and then based on the information presented in this chapter, write "T" if it is true or "F" if it is false.

1. _____ In North America, bears were responsible for an average of 46 deadly attacks per year from 2000 to 2017.

2. _____ Black bears and brown bears usually attack people more frequently than polar bears do.

3. _____ In the town of Arviat, Canada, the Halloween event of trick-or-treating has been canceled ever since 2015 due to polar bears.

4. _____ Bears kill more people in North America than tigers do in various parts of Asia today.

5. _____ The author argues that bear attacks are not only rare, but largely preventable as well.

Summary

Listen carefully to the audio recording for this section and fill in the blanks in the paragraph below.

Bears are revered in North America as a 1)_____ part of the natural landscape, but they are at times perceived as threats to human communities. It makes sense to fear bears in some ways, since they are obviously 2)_____ animals, easily capable of killing human beings. In the United States and Canada, however, they kill an average of three humans per year, which makes being killed by a bear 3)_____ less likely than being struck by lightning. Moreover, bears are responsible for fewer human deaths in North America than other 4)_____ are in other parts of the world, and fatalities from bear attacks pale in comparison with the number of deaths from snakes and mosquitos. The reality is that bears typically avoid humans, and so attacks are largely preventable by exercising 5)_____ when being in areas where they roam.

Discussion

Write a short response to the question below. Be prepared to discuss your answer out loud with fellow students if your instructor asks you to do so.

What animal would you most fear having to encounter in person? Please explain your answer.

....

....

....

🌐 Point of Interest

When swimming or surfing in the ocean, there is perhaps nothing that inspires as much fear as seeing a shark's dorsal fin protruding from the water. As is the case with bear attacks, shark attacks tend to get a lot of attention, but sharks actually kill relatively few humans each year. According to a study by the International Shark Attack File, there were five fatal attacks on humans by sharks worldwide in 2018, and on average six people are killed by sharks annually.

A Perfect World

How close are we to achieving world peace?

2つの世界大戦や冷戦などが終結して、一見すると今日は平和になったように思われる。しかし武力紛争は相変わらず世界中で起きており、世界平和の訪れにはまだ時間がかかりそうだ。武力衝突が起こる原因を探り、世界平和の実現に向けて解決すべきことを考察しよう。

The Arc de Triomphe in Paris is for many just a tourist spot. However, it holds deeper significance since it is dedicated to French soldiers who fought during the Revolutionary and Napoleonic wars, and it is the site of the Tomb of the Unknown Soldier from World War I.

Image credit: The author

Getting Started

To help you connect with this chapter's topic, take a moment to think about the questions below, and then write a short sentence to answer each one.

1. How often do you see news stories about military conflicts?

   _____

2. How often do you interact with international students?

   _____

3. Do you think the world will be more peaceful in twenty years?

   _____

Reading

1 Human history is rife with conflict, ranging from minor tribal skirmishes to total war between nation-states. The twentieth century in particular featured warfare on a scale that dwarfed all prior conflicts. Recognizing how devastating war had become, various countries around the world **assembled**[1] in 1945 to create the
5 United Nations, which, among other things, has served as a forum for settling disputes without resorting to war. While the world has since then fortunately not seen wars comparable to the Second World War, armed conflicts have nevertheless continued to rage in various places around the globe. It therefore seems like the very idea of world peace is something to deride as a naïve aspiration. While we are obviously not on the
10 cusp of achieving world peace, it is clear that a world without conflict is a worthwhile pursuit. To that end, taking a closer look at some of the common causes of armed conflict today can help us understand how much we have to overcome before we can even begin talking about world peace.

2 While the end of the Second World War in 1945 brought an end to the
15 most destructive series of armed conflicts ever fought, the world was plunged into a potentially even more dangerous conflict shortly afterward when the United States and the Soviet Union became embroiled in what is known as the Cold War. The two superpowers built increasingly powerful nuclear weapons and
20 stockpiled them by the thousands, raising the terrifying prospect of thermonuclear world war. After the United Kingdom, the People's Republic of China, and France
25 also developed nuclear weapons, it became clear that the world could soon end up with too many nuclear-armed countries. Some countries

American Minuteman missile silo
Image credit: National Park Service

therefore gathered to establish the Treaty on the Non-Proliferation of Nuclear Weapons
30 (NPT), which entered into force in 1970 and has now been signed by all but a handful of countries. The treaty essentially stipulates that only the first five countries that developed nuclear weapons can have them, and the treaty has been mostly effective with only a few notable exceptions.

3 The Soviet Union weakened in the late 1980s and officially dissolved at the
35 end of 1991, effectively marking the end of the Cold War. This essentially ended the threat of thermonuclear war between the two superpowers, and whereas there were

over seventy thousand nuclear weapons in the world in the 1980s, by 2019 there were only about fourteen thousand remaining. While the number of nuclear weapons has decreased dramatically, the number of active nuclear states in the world has increased. India tested nuclear weapons in 1998, for the first time since it detonated what it termed a "peaceful nuclear explosive" in 1974. Pakistan then conducted its own nuclear weapons test shortly after India's 1998 test. North Korea then conducted its first successful nuclear weapons test in 2006. As such, existing tensions between India and Pakistan, and on the Korean Peninsula, became potentially more dangerous after the Cold War ended.

4 The danger that nuclear weapons pose is obvious, and it is equally obvious how devastating war between countries can be. However, it is conventional weapons that have been responsible for most deaths in battle, and wars today are usually not between countries, but rather, between groups living within the borders of a particular country. In some cases, there are internal conflicts that involve different groups seeking to overthrow the government, which can lead to extreme violence. For instance, protests in 2011 against Syria's president sparked the beginning of the Syrian Civil War, which has led to the displacement of millions and the deaths of hundreds of thousands. In other cases, ethnic tensions within a country can lead to acts of genocide and ethnic cleansing, as was the case with Rwanda in 1993. More recently, a civil war broke out in South Sudan at the end of 2013, with some armed groups committing acts of violence against members of rival ethnic groups, which has resulted in fatalities estimated to be anywhere from tens of thousands to hundreds of thousands.

5 In the end, it is clear that world peace remains elusive. Even in the developed world where no daily violent conflicts involving militant groups take place, there are various other forms of conflict. Terrorism remains a serious threat throughout the world, and so police and military operations against potential and active organizations that threaten civilians will likely continue into the indefinite future. Territorial disputes like those between some countries in East Asia remain **sensitive**[2] issues to this day. In Europe and

世界中で見られる、人を死に至らしめる暴力のもう一つの要因について、章末の Point of Interest を読んでみよう。

the United States, the issue of mass migration to the West has seemingly polarized the public into deeply entrenched ideological positions, which has resulted in an increasingly tense and confrontational political environment. It seems, then, that conflict has thus far been an inescapable part of human existence, but it does not mean that the situation cannot improve in the future. Each new generation has the opportunity to find ways to **settle**[3] disputes peacefully, and hopefully the spread of intercultural exchanges in places like universities will help pave the way for future generations to achieve a more peaceful world.

rife「多い」 skirmish「小競り合い」 dwarf「小さく見せる」 devastating「壊滅的」 rage「荒れ狂う」 deride「あざける」 on the cusp of「まさに始まろうとする時期で」 plunge「突き落とす」 embroil「巻き込む」 stockpile「備蓄する」 thermonuclear「熱核兵器を使用した」 Treaty on the Non-Proliferation of Nuclear Weapons「核兵器の不拡散に関する条約（略称は核拡散防止条約）」 stipulate「規定する」 detonate「爆発させる」 elusive「実現が難しい」 confrontational「対立的な」 inescapable「不可避の」

Vocabulary

Use the context in the reading section to figure out the meaning of each underlined word below.

1. … countries around the world **assembled** in 1945 …
   a. gathered　　b. evaluated　　c. incorporated　d. encouraged

2. … remain **sensitive** issues …
   a. gentle　　　b. creative　　c. problematic　d. light

3. … find ways to **settle** disputes …
   a. achieve　　b. resolve　　c. donate　　　d. arrange

Comprehension

Read each statement below carefully, and then based on the information presented in this chapter, write "T" if it is true or "F" if it is false.

1. _____ Only five countries are allowed to have nuclear weapons according to the provisions of the NPT.

2. _____ The Soviet Union officially dissolved in 1989, which marked the official end of the Cold War.

3. _____ The most devastating conflicts today are still those that are fought between different countries.

4. _____ The Syrian Civil War has resulted in millions of people being displaced and hundreds of thousands of deaths.

5. _____ According to the author, there are so many conflicts around the world today that there is no hope for the world to become more peaceful.

Summary

Listen carefully to the audio recording for this section and fill in the blanks in the paragraph below.

In comparison with the great 1)_____ of the twentieth century like World War I, World War II, and the Cold War, the world today seems more peaceful. The end of the Cold War, for instance, has resulted in a dramatic 2)_____ in the number of nuclear weapons in the world. However, the number of active nuclear states has increased, and many different conflicts have 3)_____ out since the end of the Cold War. Some of the conflicts that erupted after the Cold War have been particularly brutal, and often involve 4)_____ groups fighting one another within the borders of a particular country. As such, while the 5)_____ of world peace is obviously enticing, it is clearly not something that we will attain anytime soon.

Discussion

Write a short response to the question below. Be prepared to discuss your answer out loud with fellow students if your instructor asks you to do so.

What international conflict have you learned about in the news recently? Please provide a few details.

....

....

....

🌐 Point of Interest

Acts of violence committed by individuals also stand in the way of achieving peace in the world. For example, in 2015, according to the World Health Organization, there were 470,000 homicide victims, and homicide rates varied by country: 5.3 homicides per 100,000 people in the United States, 85.7 per 100,000 in Honduras, 26.2 per 100,000 in South Africa, 0.9 per 100,000 in France, and 0.3 per 100,000 in Japan.

Modern Frankenstein

Will genetic engineering change life as we know it?

遺伝子工学は、SF 作品のテーマとして扱われることも多いが、『ジュラシック・パーク』や『ガタカ』が描く未来像の実現につながるかもしれないような研究が、現在すでに進められている。遺伝子工学は期待が持てる研究科学分野であるが、倫理面や安全面において問題を引き起こす可能性もある。人間と環境に責任を持った遺伝子研究とは、どうあるべきであろうか。

Farming is often associated with a traditional way of life and pastoral scenes such as this one. However, industrial farming today often relies on antibiotics, chemical pesticides, and perhaps most controversially, genetically modified crops.

Image credit: The author

Getting Started

To help you connect with this chapter's topic, take a moment to think about the questions below, and then write a short sentence to answer each one.

1. What movie have you seen that covers the topic of genetics?

   _____

2. What extinct animal species would you like to see brought back to life?

   _____

3. How do you feel about eating genetically modified food?

   _____

Reading

08 CD

1 Genetic engineering is a popular theme in science fiction. In the 1990 novel *Jurassic Park*, for example, scientists acquire the genetic information of several long-extinct dinosaur species, like Tyrannosaurus rex, and bring them back to life. By way of another example, the 1997 film *Gattaca* presents a future society wherein most parents who decide to procreate rely on genetic engineering to select the best possible genetic traits for their offspring. These visions of the future currently seem out of reach, but there is already

絶滅した動物を復活
させるために実際に
行われた試みについ
て、章末の Point of
Interest を読んでみ
よう。

5

work in progress that could very well end up making some of these visions partly true. As we will see in this chapter, though genetic engineering can offer the promise of a 10 better life, its amazing power to **transform**[1] life as we know it also raises some serious concerns about issues relating to not only ethics, but safety as well.

09 CD

2 One of the biggest concerns surrounding genetic research today involves the use of gene editing on human beings. There are two forms of gene editing, one of which has opened up promising opportunities in medicine, while the other has 15 raised concerns about the future of the human species. The first type is called somatic genetic modification, which involves altering existing genes or adding genes in the cells of a living person. This is primarily used in gene therapy, which uses genes instead of drugs to treat serious illnesses. For example, when a mutated gene is causing a disease, replacing it with a properly functioning copy of that gene can cure the illness 20 without using powerful pharmaceuticals that may have harsh side effects. This form of treatment is still in the experimental stage, however, meaning that relatively few illnesses can currently be treated with such an approach.

10 CD

3 The second type of gene editing is called germline genetic modification, and it is especially controversial when it comes to the prospect of applying it to human 25 beings. It involves modifying genetic code at the embryonic stage of development, and since genes modified in this way are inheritable, these genetic changes would be passed on to offspring. Germline genetic modification would therefore essentially mean creating genetically modified human beings. Ideally, such technology could identify and deal with problematic genes that cause terrible illnesses, like mutations in BRCA1 30 and BRCA2 that result in a significantly higher risk of developing breast cancer, for example, or mutations in the CFTR gene that can cause cystic fibrosis. The fear, however, is that this technology will lead to "designer babies" with altered inheritable traits, relating to things like intelligence and appearance. This would in all likelihood result in a situation where wealthy families could afford to have their offspring literally 35 genetically advantaged, while poorer families would have children who lack these advantages.

4 Another major concern surrounding genetic research today is the creation of genetically modified organisms, which involves altering an organism's genetic makeup by transferring genes from one organism to another. For example, a gene from the bacterium Bacillus thuringiensis (Bt) can be added to a plant's genetic code, which then leads that plant to produce a toxin that makes it more resistant to insects. Such modifications can obviously prove invaluable when applied to crops that serve as food. There is always the possibility, however, that raising genetically modified crops could result in unintended consequences to the ecosystem, and that consuming such crops could pose threats to human health that have yet to be discovered. In response to these concerns, the international community established the Cartagena

Insects destroying crops
Image credit: @iStockphoto

Protocol on Biosafety to the Convention on Biological Diversity, which outlines rules for transporting and using living modified organisms. Among other things, it stipulates certain requirements for **proper**[2] documentation to ensure that countries have information about any genetic modifications made to living organisms that they import. There are now 171 signatories, but some of the biggest exporters of agricultural products, including Australia, Canada, and the United States, have not signed.

5 Mary Shelley's novel *Frankenstein* serves as a good cautionary tale when it comes to how we should view genetic research today. Shelley's novel touches on a number of themes about humanity and society, but one theme is especially relevant here: the **potentially**[3] dangerous consequences of scientific progress. Dr. Victor Frankenstein discovers how to bring inanimate matter to life, and proceeds to create a human being. Unfortunately, the being he creates turns out to be physically hideous. Dr. Frankenstein is overwhelmed with feelings of regret and revulsion, so he flees, and the monster he created goes off alone into the countryside. It is a tragic turn of events, for despite the monster's hideous appearance, he was impressionable, innocent, and child-like. After being rejected by society, though, he turns vicious, and seeks to get revenge on his creator. "I was benevolent and good," the monster later tells Dr. Frankenstein, but "misery made me a fiend." It is easy to see genetic engineering as a dangerous scientific development with the capacity to create social upheaval and dangerously alter our environment. However, the reality is that this type of science is still relatively in its infancy, and as was the case with what happened to Dr. Frankenstein's monster, how society reacts to this technology will go a long way to determining the kind of effect it will have on the world.

Jurassic Park『ジュラシック・パーク』（マイケル・クライトン作）　long-extinct「はるか昔に絶滅した」
Tyrannosaurus rex「ティラノサウルス・レックス」　Gattaca『ガタカ』　procreate「子を産む」　offspring
「子孫」　somatic genetic modification「体細胞遺伝子組み換え」　gene therapy「遺伝子治療」　mutated「突
然変異を起こした」　pharmaceutical「薬」　germline「生殖細胞系」　genetic code「遺伝情報」　embryonic
「初期の」　inheritable「遺伝する」　BRCA1, BRCA2, CFTR（いずれも、がん抑制遺伝子）　cystic fibrosis「囊
胞（のうほう）性線維症」　genetically modified organism「遺伝子組み換え生物」　Bacillus thuringiensis「卒
倒病菌」　Cartagena Protocol on Biosafety to the Convention on Biological Diversity「生物の多様性に関
する条約のバイオセーフティーに関するカルタヘナ議定書」　signatory「条約加盟国」　Mary Shelley「メアリ
ー・シェリー（1797-1851）英国の小説家」　Frankenstein『フランケンシュタイン』（1818）　cautionary「教
訓物語」　hideous「醜い」　overwhelm「打ちのめす」　revulsion「嫌悪感」　impressionable「感受性豊かな」
upheaval「大変動」

Vocabulary

Use the context in the reading section to figure out the meaning of each underlined word below.

1. … power to **transform** life …
   　　　a. change　　b. excite　　c. create　　d. guide

2. … certain requirements for **proper** documentation …
   　　　a. interesting　b. easy　　c. detailed　　d. correct

3. … the **potentially** dangerous consequences of …
   　　　a. virtually　　b. certainly　　c. truly　　d. possibly

Comprehension

Read each statement below carefully, and then based on the information presented in this chapter, write "T" if it is true or "F" if it is false.

1. _____ In the movie *Gattaca*, genetic engineers acquire the genetic information of extinct dinosaurs and bring them back to life.

2. _____ Somatic gene modification is used primarily to treat serious illnesses by means of gene therapy.

3. _____ Germline genetic modification results in genetic changes that are actually inheritable.

4. _____ Genetically modified food can offer certain benefits, but some people worry about possible unintended consequences to the ecosystem.

5. _____ The author argues that genetic engineering is dangerous like Dr. Frankenstein's monster.

Summary

Listen carefully to the audio recording for this section and fill in the blanks in the paragraph below.

Genetic engineering is a 1)_____ field in the sciences, but it is one that also offers some potentially troubling prospects. On the one hand, gene editing has opened up 2)_____ in medicine to treat diseases by means of somatic gene modification, which could spare patients from the horrible side effects of certain pharmaceuticals. On the other hand, there is growing concern that gene modification could be used to 3)_____ human genes at the embryonic stage, which could produce inheritable beneficial traits, and could lead to a situation where the wealthy literally become privileged at the genetic level. Genetic modification is also transforming crops used for food, which can increase food supplies, but also 4)_____ expose the environment to unintended consequences. Ultimately, how genetic engineering will 5)_____ society comes down to how responsibly genetic research is applied to people and the environment.

Discussion

Write a short response to the question below. Be prepared to discuss your answer out loud with fellow students if your instructor asks you to do so.

What do you think about gene editing at the embryonic stage? Please explain your answer.

....

....

....

🌐 Point of Interest

Finding viable dinosaur genetic information from millions of years ago seems impossible, but it is possible to get the genetic information of some species that went extinct more recently. For instance, efforts are underway to bring back the woolly mammoth. One plan to accomplish this involves inserting mammoth genes, derived from dead mammoth tissues that have been preserved in ice for thousands of years, into the DNA sequence of Asian elephants to create a mammoth-elephant hybrid.

Tinted Lenses

Is it possible to be truly objective?

人間は、いろいろな解釈が可能な物事と、個人の解釈にゆだねられるべきでは
ない物事の両方に、主観的な判断を下す傾向があるようだ。完全に客観的にな
ることは事実上不可能かもしれないが、間違った判断をしたときにはそれを認
めようと努めることはできる。非理性的な考え方である認知バイアスの例を考
察しながら、ある行動を取った理由を考えることの重要性を理解しよう。

A cognitive bias known as the gambler's fallacy leads people to believe that past results affect future events even when it involves random chance. In a city like Las Vegas, that can be a costly mindset since it can lead people to miscalculate their odds of winning while gambling.

Image credit: The author

Getting Started

To help you connect with this chapter's topic, take a moment to think about the questions below, and then write a short sentence to answer each one.

1. If you flip a coin, what are the odds that it will land on the heads side?

   _____

2. How often do you trust your gut feeling over more rational calculations?

   _____

3. Do you consider yourself an optimist, a pessimist, or a little of both?

   _____

Reading

1 Much of what happens in life is open to interpretation, and whether they realize it or not, most people continuously make subjective judgments about the world around them. Personal experiences and preferences have a sizeable influence on how people view a wide variety of things, ranging from political issues and the character traits of other people, to things that actually should not be subject to interpretation, like probabilities and the laws of nature. Though it is virtually impossible to be completely objective with regard to most issues in life, it is possible to at least strive to recognize instances when one's judgment is demonstrably flawed. An obvious example of flawed judgment involves what are called cognitive biases, which are essentially irrational ways of thinking about certain aspects of the world around us. There are many different cognitive biases, but examining even just a few examples can help provide an overall **impression**[1] of how they can distort a person's view of the world around him or her. Let us therefore take a closer look at a few cognitive biases in order to understand why it is important for people to think about the reasons that lead them to act as they do.

2 One notable cognitive bias is called confirmation bias, which refers to a way of thinking that leads people to focus on information that supports their preconceptions, while dismissing information that contradicts those preconceptions. For instance, let us consider a simple example where a few isolated incidents in the distant past have led Michael to view Tom as a clumsy person. Michael and Tom are walking down the street together one morning on their way to work, as they do every weekday, and Tom suddenly stumbles and falls down. Michael immediately thinks to himself: "typical clumsy Tom." However, given that they walk down the street together on their way to work every day, without incident, Michael is letting this one incident reinforce his preexisting view of Tom, while ignoring all of the other days that Tom walks without stumbling.

3 Another type of cognitive bias is what's known as the gambler's fallacy. This involves situations where someone uses past results to make predictions about future events that involve completely random chance. A coin toss serves as a perfect example, since a coin toss always has a fifty percent chance of being heads and a fifty percent chance of being tails. If someone flips a coin and it lands heads, what are the odds that the next coin flip will land tails? The correct answer is of course fifty percent. If someone flips a coin ten times, and in all ten instances the coin comes up heads, what are the odds that the next flip will come up tails? The answer is again fifty percent. Some people, however, may be **inclined**[2] to

> コイントスの確率について、章末の Point of Interest を読んで、さらに理解を深めよう。

think that if the coin has landed heads multiple times in a row, then it is surely due to land tails next time, and this kind of irrational way of thinking is a perfect example of the gambler's fallacy.

17 **CD**

4 Finally, another cognitive bias is called illusory superiority, which essentially means that some people believe that they are better than average at particular tasks 5 when they in fact are not. This has been experimentally confirmed numerous times, for researchers have conducted various studies wherein most of the participants believe that they are better at a particular task than the majority of the other participants. This means that some of them are clearly overestimating their abilities. What is known as the Dunning-Kruger effect is one specific type of illusory superiority, and it refers 10 to a phenomenon where people overestimate their standing relative to others with regard to intellectual tasks. Based on studies of university students who were each asked to evaluate their own performance, those who performed poorly tended to believe that they were above average. Conversely, those who performed well tended to underestimate their standing in comparison with others, likely due to a belief that 15 since it is easy for them, it must be easy for others.

18 **CD**

5 After looking at these three cognitive biases, it is clear that people can indeed perceive certain aspects of the world around them in distorted ways, which can in some instances lead to serious problems. For example, if people are gambling a lot of money and believe that the winning roll of the dice is imminent because they have rolled the dice so many times already, they can end up in serious financial trouble. Similarly, it does not seem all that bad if someone misjudges his friend's level of clumsiness. However, this kind of bias can **foster**[3] discriminatory attitudes when someone takes an example on the news that involves people from a particular group and concludes that it serves as proof that his or her negative views of that group are correct. Finally, having people think too highly of themselves may seem like just a minor personality issue. It can unfortunately be a dangerous cognitive bias

The Thinker, by French sculptor Auguste Rodin
Image credit: The author

when it leads people to do things beyond their abilities like, for example, drive faster 35 than they can handle. It is therefore clear that cognitive biases can have a profoundly negative impact on the way people think and act, and so it is important that people stay vigilant about making sure to reflect on the reasons why they think and act the way they do.

demonstrably「明らかに」 flawed「間違っている」 preconception「先入観」 clumsy「不器用な」 fallacy「誤った考え」 illusory superiority 「幻想的優位」 Dunning-Kruger effect 「ダニング・クルーガー効果」 imminent「差し迫った」 vigilant「用心している」

Vocabulary

Use the context in the reading section to figure out the meaning of each underlined word below.

1. … provide an overall **impression** of how …

    a. sense   b. impact   c. mark   d. statement

2. … may be **inclined** to think that …

    a. forwarded   b. told   c. determined   d. likely

3. … this kind of bias can **foster** discriminatory attitudes …

    a. promote   b. care   c. eliminate   d. feature

Comprehension

Read each statement below carefully, and then based on the information presented in this chapter, write "T" if it is true or "F" if it is false.

1. _____ In the case of confirmation bias, people focus on information that supports their pre-existing views.

2. _____ In the case of the gambler's fallacy, people ignore past results and continue betting as if the past results had not happened.

3. _____ Illusory superiority refers to cases where people mistakenly overestimate their abilities in comparison with those of others.

4. _____ The Dunning-Kruger effect refers to people with higher abilities in intellectual tasks who think they are superior to others.

5. _____ The author argues that there could be serious repercussions if people do not think about the reasons for why they do what they do.

Summary

Listen carefully to the audio recording for this section and fill in the blanks in the paragraph below.

Human beings are seemingly naturally inclined to make subjective judgments about things that are open to interpretation, like morality, political issues, and aesthetic 1)_____. In some cases, however, certain cognitive biases lead people to make subjective judgments about things that are 2)_____ not subject to interpretation. Many different cognitive biases can affect the way people think and the way they 3)_____ reality, including confirmation bias, the gambler's fallacy, and illusory superiority. Though the details of these cognitive biases vary 4)_____, they all have one thing in common, which is that they are all modes of thinking that lead people to have distorted views of the world around them. These modes of thinking may seem 5)_____ on the surface, but they can lead people to make bad decisions that can have serious consequences.

Discussion

Write a short response to the question below. Be prepared to discuss your answer out loud with fellow students if your instructor asks you to do so.

What is the best example of confirmation bias that you have experienced or observed? Please provide a few basic details.

....

....

....

🌐 Point of Interest

The odds of a coin landing heads ten times in a row are only one out of 1,024. If someone were to begin flipping a coin repeatedly in an effort to achieve ten heads in a row, and had already failed 1,023 times to get ten in a row, what are the odds that he or she will get ten heads in a row on the next try? The correct answer is still, of course, one out of 1,024.

Get Well Soon

How are X-rays affecting healthcare today?

この数世紀の間に、医学の分野は飛躍的に変化した。診断医学を劇的に変え医用画像処理の先駆けとなったのは、1895 年に X 線を発見したドイツの物理学者ヴィルヘルム・レントゲンである。X 線を用いた医用画像処理の有用性と問題点を見てみよう。

The discovery of X-rays has had a profound impact of the field of medicine. Today, X-ray technology plays a vital role in not only diagnosing bone injuries, but also serious medical problems like strokes and various types of cancer.

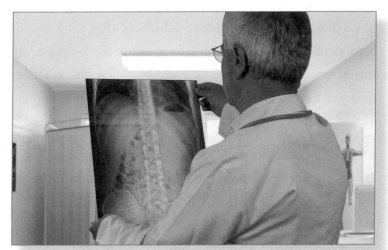

Image credit: @iStockphoto

Getting Started

To help you connect with this chapter's topic, take a moment to think about the questions below, and then write a short sentence to answer each one.

1. Approximately how many CT scanners do you think there are in Japan?

   _____

2. How many X-rays do you think you have taken throughout your life?

   _____

3. Which do you think is better: an MRI scan or a CT scan?

   _____

Reading

1 The field of medicine has changed dramatically over the last few centuries. For instance, British physician Edward Jenner's vaccine for smallpox in 1796 paved the way for vaccination protocols that now help prevent numerous contagious illnesses, ranging from measles to rabies. In 1864, French biologist Louis Pasteur developed a process known as pasteurization, which is crucial for helping prevent foodborne illnesses. 5 Another radical breakthrough came in 1928, when Scottish biologist Alexander Fleming created the first effective antibiotic, penicillin, which spared countless lives from the ravages of bacterial infections. While specialists in medicine or biology were responsible for all of these medical breakthroughs, it is a German physicist, Wilhelm Röntgen, who helped transform diagnostic medicine and usher in the era of medical 10 imaging when he discovered X-rays in 1895. Medical imaging based on X-rays has proven invaluable for **detecting**[1] illnesses and injuries, but as we will see in this chapter, it also raises some serious concerns.

2 The first X-rays were only able to reveal basic bone structures and the presence of foreign objects, but standard X-ray imaging technology today can now reveal 15 intricate details about bones, and even some basic details about internal organs. The most notable advance in X-ray imaging, however, came with the development of computed tomography (CT). The first CT scanner, built in 1971, was only used to create images of the brain, and then in 1975 the 20 first CT scanner designed to examine the entire body was introduced. A CT scan involves a series of X-ray slices of a specific part of the body, and computer programs can assemble these slices into three-dimensional images. Today's CT scanners can produce incredibly detailed images and have become **vital**[2] tools for detecting things like internal injuries, damaged blood vessels, and diseases like cancer. 25

> 日本にある CT スキャナーの台数について、章末の Point of Interest を読んでみよう。

3 There is another type of scan that can create highly detailed images of the body, including three-dimensional images: magnetic resonance imaging (MRI). This imaging technology is, generally speaking, superior when it comes to examining soft tissues like the brain, while CT scans are superior for examining bony structures. Regardless of image quality, CT scans are often the preferred choice for several reasons. 30 For one thing, MRI machines are more expensive, so fewer medical facilities have them, which typically results in longer wait times and higher costs. MRI scans are also unpleasant for patients, who are confined in a relatively tight space, and subject to incredibly loud noise over the course of the scanning process. Finally, CT scans are far more suitable for emergency situations, when doctors suspect, for example, an 35 immediately life-threatening condition like a possible stroke or severe internal injuries from a car accident. CT scans are usually preferable in such circumstances because they are faster than MRI scans, and patient movement does not affect CT images as much as with MRI images. Moreover, life-supporting medical equipment with metal parts can typically accompany patients while getting a CT scan, whereas this is not possible with an MRI scan since it uses magnetic fields.

23 CD

4 Aside from differences in imaging quality, CT scans have one significant disadvantage. MRI uses radio waves and magnetic fields to generate images, whereas CT scanners use X-rays that expose patients to ionizing radiation, which can potentially raise someone's risk of developing cancer later in life. A single chest X-ray, for example, exposes patients to approximately 0.02 millisieverts, which is only a negligible dose of radiation, but a chest CT scan exposes patients to approximately seven millisieverts. Positron emission tomography (PET) is another type of scan that can yield useful diagnostic information, and it is often done simultaneously with a CT scan, in which case it is simply called a PET/ CT scan. A PET scan involves injecting

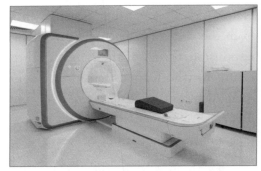

A magnetic resonance imaging (MRI) scanner
Image credit: @iStockphoto

a patient with a radiotracer, which is a small amount of radioactive material like F-18 fluorodeoxyglucose (FDG). It is then possible to scan the body for radioactive emissions from the radiotracer, which can offer valuable diagnostic information. For example, cancerous tumors readily absorb certain radiotracers, and so if a PET scan detects that an injected radiotracer accumulates in one specific part of the body, then it indicates the likely presence of a tumor. The downside, of course, is that these scans expose patients to even more radiation.

24 CD

5 The bottom line is that imaging tests are vital tools that can help detect illnesses early, thereby increasing the chances of finding a cure or at least slowing down a disease's progression. This potential benefit, however, must be weighed against the risks of radiation exposure from certain kinds of scans. In some cases, doctors order CT scans, and even PET/CT scans, for patients whose symptoms are not serious enough to **warrant**[3] such tests. There are even instances when completely asymptomatic individuals seek out full-body CT or PET/CT for the purposes of screening for diseases. In asymptomatic individuals, the small risk from the amount of ionizing radiation from such a test seemingly outweighs the very small possibility that it will detect a serious illness. When someone has menacing symptoms, on the other hand, the increased likelihood of discovering a potentially life-threatening illness usually outweighs the small risk of developing cancer later in life. In this way, then, CT and PET/CT are life-saving tools when used properly, but in rare cases can result in healthy people actually developing the cancerous illnesses that they were screening for by getting unnecessarily exposed to ionizing radiation while screening for them.

Edward Jenner「エドワード・ジェンナー（1749-1823）」 **vaccination**「予防接種」 **measles**「はしか」 **rabies**「狂犬病」 **Louis Pasteur**「ルイ・パスツール（1822-1895）」 **pasteurization**「低温殺菌」 **foodborne illness**「食中毒」 **breakthrough**「飛躍的な進展」 **Alexander Fleming**「アレキサンダー・フレミング（1881-1955）」 **antibiotic**「抗生物質」 **Wilhelm Röntgen**「ヴィルヘルム・レントゲン（1845-1923）」 **medical imaging**「医用画像処理」 **invaluable**「計り知れないほど貴重な」 **computed tomography**「コンピューター X 線断層撮影法」 **magnetic resonance imaging**「磁気共鳴画像法」 **stroke**「脳卒中」 **magnetic field**「磁場」 **ionizing radiation**「電離放射線」 **millisievert**「ミリシーベルト（放射線量の単位）」 **dose**「線量」 **positron emission tomography**「陽電子放射断層撮影法」 **radiotracer**「放射性追跡子」 **radioactive**「放射性の」 **fluorodeoxyglucose**「フルオロデオキシグルコース」 **cancerous**「がん性の」 **tumor**「腫瘍」 **downside**「欠点」 **asymptomatic**「無症候の」 **outweigh**「より重要である」

Vocabulary

Use the context in the reading section to figure out the meaning of each underlined word below.

1. … invaluable for **detecting** illnesses …
   - a. treating   b. fixing   c. covering   d. discovering
2. … imaging tests are **vital** tools …
   - a. interesting   b. essential   c. lively   d. creative
3. … are not serious enough to **warrant** such …
   - a. create   b. justify   c. monitor   d. determine

Comprehension

Read each statement below carefully, and then based on the information presented in this chapter, write "T" if it is true or "F" if it is false.

1. _____ Wilhelm Röntgen was a German scientist specializing in the field of medicine and in the field of biology.

2. _____ Magnetic resonance imaging generates better images of soft tissues, and so MRI is always the preferred option when scanning people.

3. _____ Computed tomography scans generate ionizing radiation, which can potentially cause cancer.

4. _____ Positron emission tomography involves injecting patients with a radiotracer, and is often done simulateneously with a CT scan.

5. _____ The author argues that having people get CT scans to screen for cancer before developing symptoms is a good idea.

Summary

Listen carefully to the audio recording for this section and fill in the blanks in the paragraph below.

Wilhelm Röntgen's discovery of X-rays in 1895 forever changed the field of medicine by 1)_____ in the era of medical imaging. Whereas X-rays could 2)_____ only reveal simple things like broken bones, X-ray technology today can reveal a great deal more, including some basic visual details about internal organs. X-ray technology has even led to the 3)_____ of computed tomography scanning, commonly known simply as CT scanning. CT scans can create three-dimensional images and are 4)_____ tools for detecting life-threatening injuries and illnesses, like tumors, strokes, and damaged internal organs. The main drawback when it comes to CT scans is that patients get 5)_____ to ionizing radiation, and so it is important that patients and doctors make sure that the benefits of getting such scans are likely to outweigh the risks.

Discussion

Write a short response to the question below. Be prepared to discuss your answer out loud with fellow students if your instructor asks you to do so.

In your opinion, what is the biggest advantage that CT scans have over MRI scans? Please explain your answer.

....

....

....

🌐 Point of Interest

According to 2014-2017 data from the Organisation for Economic Co-operation and Development (OECD), Japan has more CT scanners than any other country, with a little over one hundred CT scanners per one million people. This is more than double the per capita number in the United States, which has forty-three per million. The country with the second highest number of CT scanners is Australia, with sixty-four per million.

The Need for Speed

Chapter 15

Is it time to restrict how fast cars can go?

高級スポーツカーのみならず、セダンのような普通の車でも法定速度よりかなり早く走行できるものがある。自動車メーカーは、なぜ法定速度よりはるかに速く走行できる製品を製造しているのだろうか。スピード違反による交通事故が極めて多いことを考えると、メーカーは車の最高速度を制限することを検討する時期ではないだろうか。

When people drive faster than legally allowed, they increase the likelihood of causing traffic accidents. It is therefore necessary to enforce traffic rules, and so those who commit infractions while driving always face the risk of being pulled over by police.

Image credit: The author

Getting Started

To help you connect with this chapter's topic, take a moment to think about the questions below, and then write a short sentence to answer each one.

1. How often do you see cars on the road seemingly going too fast?

   _____

2. What is your favorite movie that features exciting car scenes?

   _____

3. What is your favorite type of car?

   _____

Reading

26

1 According to the International Organization of Motor Vehicle Manufacturers, over seventy million cars were sold in 2017, which represents an increase of over one million sales from the previous year, and an increase of over twenty-five million sales in comparison with sales in 2005. Needless to say, the automotive industry is huge, and as with most industries, advertising for their products is pervasive. Car advertisements typically highlight comfort, style, and safety, among other things. In some cases, one of those other things is speed. Some ads showcase a car's performance, as it seemingly roars down beautiful open roads, and then navigates tight turns along seaside cliffs. The reality, however, is that most cars end up in predominantly urban environments where speeding is exceptionally dangerous. Though traffic laws obviously set speed limits, some people nevertheless drive too fast, an act that is often a factor in car accidents. This raises the question: is it time for manufacturers to restrict the maximum speed on the automobiles they sell?

27

2 Popular sports cars by manufacturers like Lamborghini can reach speeds that actually come close to, or even exceed, the top speeds reached in NASCAR (The National Association for Stock Car Auto Racing) races in the United States, which usually hit around 320 kilometers per hour. Some luxury sports cars can even go over 400 kilometers per hour. While such cars are relatively rare, even a regular car like a sedan or a sport utility vehicle can reach speeds well in excess of 160 kilometers per hour, which is still over the highest posted speed limits in countries like Japan, Canada, and the United States. It therefore seems strange that people can legally own such fast cars in countries where speed limits do not allow anything close to such high speeds.

> 量産車の中で、世界最速のスピードを出す車はどれか、章末の Point of Interest を読んでみよう。

3 One could argue that cars should not be made to go faster than what is legally allowed on public roads and highways. Why, then, have manufacturers been making such fast cars? For one thing, speed sells, and so making cars that top out at speeds that people consider overly safe and dull would likely hurt a vehicle's marketability. There is also the reality that speed limits do not completely **regulate**[1] traffic flow. On many American highways, for example, it is common to have the flow of traffic a bit over the speed limit. Having new cars with built-in restrictions that do not allow drivers to go over the speed limit could initially prove hazardous, since many older cars without this technology would still be on the highway dictating the flow of traffic. In short, there are times when it may be necessary to drive over the speed limit, and an argument can be made that drivers should be entrusted to use their judgment about when it might be appropriate to do so.

4 Many manufacturers actually do, to some extent, restrict the top speed of the vehicles they produce. The electronics used in automobiles today make it easier than ever for manufacturers to program a maximum allowed speed into cars. In most cases, however, the maximum speeds programmed by manufacturers are not based on traffic laws, but are instead based on a vehicle's features, like tire rating and engine capabilities. Economy class cars, for example, are simply not built to **handle**[2] high speeds, so some manufacturers set the maximum speed at around 175 kilometers per hour, which is still considerably faster than any posted speed limit in countries like Japan, Canada, and the United States. There is at least one instance, however, of manufacturers setting a maximum speed for the sake of preventing drivers from

Canadian highway with 110 km/h speed limit
Image credit: The author

going dangerously fast. There is an alleged "gentlemen's agreement" amongst some elite German car manufacturers, whereby they set the maximum speed on their high-performance automobiles at approximately 250 kilometers per hour, even though such cars can likely handle even higher speeds. This alleged agreement is to prevent overly dangerous speeds on Germany's Bundesautobahn, known simply as the autobahn in English, which is a highway system famous for having no speed limit on most segments.

5 In the end, then, this issue comes down to whether we should trust more in human judgment, or rely more on automated systems. The European Parliament's Committee on Internal Market and Consumer Protection voted in 2019 to make intelligent speed assistance mandatory on new cars in Europe beginning in 2022, which would essentially restrict a vehicle's maximum speed based on posted speed limits. If Europe does indeed implement such a rule, it raises the prospect, or specter, depending on your point of view, that speed-limiting technology could become standard elsewhere as well. Such a change could actually be all for the best, given that according to a World Health Organization report published in 2018, the number of road traffic deaths has been steadily rising, from 1.15 million in 2000 to 1.35 million in 2016. Human error is one of the biggest contributors to fatal car accidents, and the faster someone is driving, the deadlier a mistake can be. While most people do not like the idea of machines placing **restrictions**[3] on their decisions, it is important to remember that the same restrictions would apply to the countless other drivers with whom they share the road—and such restrictions could end up saving them from someone else's high-speed mistake.

International Organization of Motor Vehicle Manufacturers「国際自動車工業連合会」 **showcase**「売り込む」 **roar**「ごう音を立てて進む」 **Lamborghini**「ランボルギーニ（イタリアの自動車メーカー）」 **top out**「最高に達する」 **marketability**「市場性」 **hazardous**「危険な」 **dictate**「決める」 **alleged**「いわゆる」 **autobahn**「アウトバーン（ドイツとオーストリアの高速道路）」 **European Parliament's committee on Internal Market and Consumer Protection**「欧州議会域内市場及び消費者保護委員会」 **intelligent speed assistance**「自動速度制御支援装置（法定速度を超えて走行した場合にブレーキをかけるか減速させる装置）」 **World Health Organization**「世界保健機関」

Vocabulary

Use the context in the reading section to figure out the meaning of each underlined word below.

1. … limits do not completely **regulate** traffic …

         a. delegate   b. control   c. create   d. normalize

2. … not built to **handle** high speeds …

         a. turn   b. manage   c. alleviate   d. rotate

3. … placing **restrictions** on their decisions …

         a. consequences   b. troubles   c. problems   d. constraints

Comprehension

Read each statement below carefully, and then based on the information presented in this chapter, write "T" if it is true or "F" if it is false.

1. _____ There were a million fewer cars sold around the world in 2017 than there were sold in 2016.

2. _____ The fastest luxury sports cars have top speeds that reach around 320 kilometers per hour, which is similar to NASCAR speeds.

3. _____ Some manufacturers do restrict the top speed on some of their vehicles based on what kind of speed a particular car can handle.

4. _____ All German car manufacturers make cars as fast as possible since there are no speed limits on the autobahn.

5. _____ The author concludes that losing one's own freedom to decide how fast to drive is too high a price to pay to prevent future accidents.

Summary

Listen carefully to the audio recording for this section and fill in the blanks in the paragraph below.

With over seventy million automobiles sold in 2017 worldwide, it is clear that cars are extremely 1)_____ items to purchase. Some elite sports cars have the ability to go faster than even some race cars, and even 2)_____ automobiles like sedans typically can go considerably faster than posted speed limits. This raises serious concerns about why manufacturers are creating products that 3)_____ consumers to drive so much faster than legally allowed. Some manufacturers do restrict the maximum speed of their vehicles based on considerations like tire rating, but even then, these vehicles can still 4)_____ any posted speed limit. Given that there are so many speed-related fatal traffic accidents every day, it seems as though it is time to at least 5)_____ having manufacturers restrict the maximum speed of the automobiles they sell.

Discussion

Write a short response to the question below. Be prepared to discuss your answer out loud with fellow students if your instructor asks you to do so.

Do you think automakers should restrict the maximum speed on cars? Please explain your answer.

....

....

....

🌐 Point of Interest

In 2010, the Bugatti Veyron 16.4 Super Sport was awarded the Guinness World Record for the fastest production car. Its top speed was recorded at 268 miles per hour, which is 431 kilometers per hour. In 2017, the Koenigsegg Agera RS beat this top speed record, reaching 277.9 miles per hour, which is 444.6 kilometers per hour.

Time Travel

Chapter 16

Will it one day be possible to build a time machine?

SFのジャンルでは、タイムトラベルを扱う話がたくさんある。過去に戻ったり、未来をのぞいてみたり、現在と過去・未来を行き来したりと、時空を超えた旅は誰もが体験してみたいと思うことだろう。しかし、そもそもタイムトラベルなど、可能なのだろうか。驚いたことに、ある種のタイムトラベルは実現可能かもしれないのだ。アインシュタインの理論を見てみよう。

The name Big Ben technically refers to the Great Bell in the clocktower, but the name is often used to refer to the clock and clock tower as well. It is not only London's most iconic monument, but it is also perhaps the most famous clock in the world.

Image credit: The author

Getting Started

To help you connect with this chapter's topic, take a moment to think about the questions below, and then write a short sentence to answer each one.

1. If you could travel back in time, which time period would you visit?

   _____

2. If you could travel forward in time, what year would you visit?

   _____

3. What is your favorite fictional story that features time travel?

   _____

Reading

1 The science fiction genre is filled with stories that feature time travel. In fact, *The Time Machine*, an 1895 short novel by H. G. Wells, is one of the earliest works of science fiction. Having a time machine would enable us to travel back in time to watch historic events first-hand, for example, or to travel to the distant future to see things like human colonies on other planets. Someone could even use a time machine ₅ to change the past or get information from the future, in order to improve his or her own life in the present. Regardless of the specifics, it seems safe to say that just about everyone would love to have an opportunity to travel through time. This raises an obvious question: is time travel even remotely possible? As we will discover in this chapter, surprisingly, certain forms of time travel may indeed be possible. ₁₀

2 In 1905, Albert Einstein outlined the principles of what is known as the special theory of relativity. Taking the view that space and time are inextricably linked as four-dimensional space-time, Einstein demonstrated that the rate at which time passes varies according to one's velocity. As renowned physicist Brian Greene succinctly puts it, this theory indicates that the faster you move through space, the slower you experience the ₁₅ passage of time, and vice versa. This phenomenon is completely unnoticeable in daily life because we simply never travel at fast enough speeds, but the effects grow increasingly noticeable as velocity begins to approach the speed of light. This means that if we could build a spaceship capable of traveling at a speed

> 未来にタイムトラベルする別の方法について、章末の Point of Interest を読んでみよう。

that approaches that of light, time would **apparently**[1] slow down for those inside the ₂₀ ship relative to the passage of time experienced by those back on Earth. Someone could therefore conceivably take a roundtrip journey, and age just a few days, but find that weeks, months, or even years had elapsed on Earth, depending on how close to the speed of light the ship traveled.

₂₅

3 This is not just purely theoretical, for this theory has actually been tested multiple times. In 1971, for example, a pair of scientists placed multiple cesium atomic clocks on board an aircraft and compared them with cesium atomic clocks that remained on the ground. The results were in line with predictions based on Einstein's theory, and indeed the clocks in motion aboard the aircraft ran a minuscule fraction ₃₀ of a second slower than the stationary clocks on the ground. Though it is tempting to dismiss the results, given that it seems as though a mere fraction of a second could be just a glitch or the result of natural variations among clocks, this is virtually impossible in the case of cesium atomic clocks. These clocks essentially operate on a frequency of a little over nine billion hertz, which means that they basically "tick" over nine billion times per second. Such clocks therefore make it possible to **reliably**[2] measure ₃₅ an incredibly minute fraction of a second, and so they can measure the effects of even relatively slow speeds on the passage of time.

35 CD

4 With regard to traveling backward in time, on the other hand, current theoretical work has technically not completely closed off the possibility. In 1915, Einstein outlined what is known as the general theory of relativity, which reveals, among other things, how mass and energy warp space-time. Under certain conditions it hypothetically is possible to warp space-time so significantly that it would create what is called a "closed time-like curve," which would allow something to travel forward in space-time and loop back to its starting position in space-time. Another possibility is based on what are called "wormholes," which are theoretical tunnels that connect two different points in space-time. As a matter of common sense, however, it seems clear that traveling backward in time is simply impossible. In fact, many physicists acknowledge that these theoretical forms of backward time travel may simply be the result of mathematical quirks of current theoretical work, and some suggest that future revisions to these theories may confirm that traveling backward in time is indeed impossible.

36 CD

5 In the end, then, it seems certain that the only form of time travel that is possible involves slowing down one's own rate of time relative to the rate of time on Earth in order to essentially travel forward in time. However, we are unfortunately not even close to having the technology needed to do this. Consider that in 2018 the National Aeronautics and Space Administration (NASA) announced that its Parker Solar Probe set the record for the fastest spacecraft ever launched when it went a little over 153,000 miles per hour. Its velocity is increasing, and by 2024 it is expected to reach approximately 430,000

Rocket carrying the Parker Solar Probe
Image credit: NASA

miles per hour. This seems fast, but to have an even **moderately**[3] noticeable effect on the passage of time requires a velocity of at least 223,000,000 miles per hour, which is a third of the speed of light. Even if future generations manage to design a manned spacecraft that can travel this fast, it is worth noting that it would mean one-way time travel. Since time moves forward for everyone, just at different rates depending on their rate of motion, the people aboard such a ship would likely find significant changes to the world they left upon their return to Earth, and they would have to learn to live with these changes since there would be no way for them to roll back the clock.

The Time Machine『タイムマシーン』(1895)   H. G. Wells「ハーバート・ジョージ・ウェルズ (1866-1946)」 specific「詳細」 remotely「わずかに」 Albert Einstein「アルバート・アインシュタイン (1879-1955)」 the special theory of relativity「特殊相対性理論」 inextricably「切り離せないほどに」 space-time「時空」 velocity「速度」 Brian Greene「ブライアン・グリーン (1963-)」 succinctly「簡潔に」 conceivably「ひょっとすると」 elapse「通過する」 cesium「セシウム」 minuscule「非常に小さい」 stationary「静止している」 glitch「故障」 the general theory of relativity「一般相対性理論」 warp「ゆがめる」 closed time-like curve「時間的閉曲線」 wormhole「ワームホール」 quirk「気まぐれ」

Vocabulary

Use the context in the reading section to figure out the meaning of each underlined word below.

1. … would **apparently** slow down for …
    a. possibly   b. never   c. seemingly   d. visually

2. … make it possible to **reliably** measure …
    a. incredibly   b. eventually   c. dependably   d. truly

3. … to have an even **moderately** noticeable effect …
    a. somewhat   b. perhaps   c. extreme   d. unique

Comprehension

Read each statement below carefully, and then based on the information presented in this chapter, write "T" if it is true or "F" if it is false.

1. _____ The faster you move through space, the faster you will experience the passage of time.

2. _____ The ability to essentially travel forward in time has actually been tested with experiments that use atomic clocks.

3. _____ It is clearly not possible to travel backward in time, yet current theoretical work cannot rule out this form of time travel.

4. _____ A closed time-like curve could allow people to travel from the current time period back to events from centuries ago.

5. _____ The author argues that the Parker Space Probe serves as a good sign of how close we are to one day achieving time travel.

Summary

Listen carefully to the audio recording for this section and fill in the blanks in the paragraph below.

The prospect of being able to create a machine that would 1)_____ people to travel through time is undeniably intriguing, but it has long seemed like something purely out of science fiction. According to Albert Einstein's special theory of relativity, however, there is one way for people to 2)_____ travel to the future. According to this theory, the faster someone moves, the slower time 3)_____ for that person relative to the rate of time for others who are not moving as fast. As exciting as this prospect seems, however, we do not yet have the technology needed to 4)_____ a fast enough speed to do this. Even if we one day 5)_____ the technology to travel fast enough to do so, someone who does this cannot undo it, and so it would effectively be a one-way trip to the future.

Discussion

Write a short response to the question below. Be prepared to discuss your answer out loud with fellow students if your instructor asks you to do so.

If you could travel a hundred years into the future, using a high-speed spacecraft, would you do it? Please explain your answer.

....

....

....

🌐 Point of Interest

Gravity can also affect the passage of time. The stronger the effects of gravity, the slower the passage of time. This means that if it were possible to take a ship to a place where the effects of gravity are extraordinarily strong, like the edge of a black hole, it would be possible for those aboard the ship to age only a brief period of time relative to how much people would age back on Earth.

The Great Unknown

How big is the universe?

この5世紀の間に、人類は宇宙に関して多くのことを知ることになった。地球は宇宙の中心だと信じられていたのが、今では無数の銀河系の中の1つの銀河にある、そのまた無数にある星の中の1つの星の軌道を回る惑星である、というように。宇宙の大きさが明らかになるのはいつだろうか。そもそも、宇宙の大きさは測れるだろうか。

With a seemingly endless selection of galaxies to gaze upon through our telescopes, one of the greatest sources of fascination when it comes to the universe is its sheer size, which may well be infinite.

Image credit: @iStockphoto

Getting Started

To help you connect with this chapter's topic, take a moment to think about the questions below, and then write a short sentence to answer each one.

1. How often do you look up at night to stare at the stars?

   _____

2. How many galaxies do you think there are in the universe?

   _____

3. How old do you think the universe is?

   _____

Reading

1 Over the course of five centuries, our place in the universe has gotten smaller and smaller. In the 1500s, for instance, Earth was widely believed to be at the center of the universe, until Polish astronomer Nicolaus Copernicus formulated the heliocentric model of the heavens, which states that Earth
5 orbits the Sun. In the centuries that followed, astronomers increasingly speculated that the Sun was not the center of the universe, but actually just one of countless other stars in the galaxy. Then in the 1920s, American astronomer
10 Edwin Hubble's observations confirmed that our galaxy, the Milky Way, was just one of many other galaxies. Earth thus went from being at the center of the universe, to now being just a planet that orbits a star that is just one of
15 countless others in our galaxy, which is itself just one of billions of galaxies. An ongoing stream

Hubble Space Telescope
Image credit: NASA

of discoveries has therefore led mankind to continually find that the universe is bigger than previously thought, and this may lead some people to wonder about when we will finally know the true size of the universe. As this chapter reveals, however, figuring out
20 the size of the universe may ultimately be an impossible task.

39

2 In 1927, a Belgian priest and physicist named Georges Lemaître came up with a radical proposal at the time: the universe is not static, but rather, it is expanding. Not only that, but since it is expanding, Lemaître concluded that the universe had to have been smaller in the past. Taken to its logical conclusion, this means that the universe
25 had to have been **condensed**[1] into one spot at some point in the distant past. Lemaître therefore theorized that an explosion must have launched the universe's expansion from this one spot, and this view became known as the Big Bang theory. Two years later, Hubble published his findings that provided empirical evidence that the universe is indeed expanding. The discovery in 1965 of what is known as cosmic microwave
30 background (CMB) radiation, which is a remnant of what happened right after the "bang" nearly fourteen billion years ago, helped further solidify the Big Bang theory as the leading explanation for how the universe has come to be as it is today.

40

3 Returning to our question about the size of the universe, it is important to first make a crucial distinction between the observable universe and the entire universe.
35 Our understanding of the universe is limited by what our instruments can observe, and so our understanding of the universe is actually just an understanding of the observable

universe. As for the size of the observable universe, the most distant CMB signals that we are now observing on Earth took almost fourteen billion years to reach us, meaning that they have traveled nearly fourteen billion light years to get here. The universe is expanding, however, and so astronomers estimate that the areas from where these signals originated nearly fourteen billion years ago are now a little over forty-six billion 5 light years away. Since these distant CMB signals are found pretty evenly distributed in every direction from Earth, it means that the current diameter of the observable universe is approximately ninety-three billion light years.

41 🎧CD

4 What lies beyond the **boundaries**[2] of the observable universe, though, remains a mystery. Perhaps there is more of the same, and the universe as we know it is simply 10 far larger than current estimates. Perhaps there is a vast infinite void. Or perhaps, and most intriguingly, there are other universes, meaning that the universe as we know it is just one of countless others in what has been dubbed the "multiverse." A number of scientists, including world-renowned physicist Stephen Hawking, have written that it is 15 quite possible that our universe is indeed part of a multiverse. Many different multiverse theories have been put forward, but

> これまでに発見された最も遠い銀河系について、章末のPoint of Interest を読んでみよう。

one of the simplest is that multiple big bangs have occurred throughout an infinite expanse, and so there could be an infinite number of bubbles that are like what we call the observable universe. Regardless of the details, if the multiverse theory is accurate, 20 it could mean that the observable universe is just an infinitesimally small part of an infinite number of other universes.

42 🎧CD

5 All told, then, modern astronomy is continually making discoveries about the universe, and so we will likely soon find that the observable universe is even bigger than current estimates. Nevertheless, we will never be able to learn the true extent of 25 the entire universe since its rate of expansion is accelerating, and it likely **spans**[3] out infinitely in some fashion. This is hardly the only feature that remains a mystery since many questions about the universe remain unanswered, and some touch on even more tantalizing issues. For example, as the German philosopher Gottfried Leibniz put it, why is there something instead of nothing? We can rephrase this by asking: why does 30 the universe exist at all? It is a question that has likely intrigued mankind since the birth of civilization, but this question is essentially impossible to answer. The universe is therefore clearly a source of great mystery, and as frustrating as questions like these are, they can at least help fuel our sense of wonder when we look up at the nighttime sky and peer into the apparently endless depths of the cosmos.

NOTES ....

Nicolaus Copernicus「ニコラウス・コペルニクス (1473-1543)」 **Edwin Hubble**「エドウィン・ハッブル（1889-1953)」 **galaxy**「銀河系」 **Milky Way**「銀河」 **Georges Lemaître**「ジョルジュ・ルメートル

(1894-1966)」 **Big Bang theory**「ビッグバン理論」 **empirical**「実証的」 **cosmic microwave background radiation**「宇宙マイクロ波背景放射」 **remnant**「残存物」 **diameter**「直径」 **void**「宇宙空間」 **multiverse**「多宇宙」 **Stephen Hawking**「スティーヴン・ホーキング (1942-2018)」 **infinitesimally**「最小限度まで」 **tantalizing**「興味をそそる」 **Gottfried Leibniz**「ゴットフリート・ライプニッツ (1646-1716)」 **intrigue**「興味をそそる」 **fuel**「あおる」

Vocabulary

Use the context in the reading section to figure out the meaning of each underlined word below.

1. … had to have been **condensed** into one spot …
   - a. mixed   b. found   c. compressed   d. made
2. … beyond the **boundaries** of the observable universe …
   - a. edges   b. frames   c. connections   d. features
3. … it likely **spans** out infinitely …
   - a. extends   b. moves   c. experiences   d. exerts

Comprehension

Read each statement below carefully, and then based on the information presented in this chapter, write "T" if it is true or "F" if it is false.

1. _____ Edwin Hubble published empirical data that helped Georges Lemaître come up with the idea that the universe is expanding.

2. _____ The size of the observable universe is currently believed to be a little over forty-six billion light years in diameter.

3. _____ The entire universe may be far bigger than ninety-three billion light years in diameter, and could even be infinitely vast.

4. _____ The multiverse is a speculative theory that has no support among respected physicists.

5. _____ The author argues that it is frustrating that we do not know the size of the universe, but expects that science will discover it soon.

Summary

Listen carefully to the audio recording for this section and fill in the blanks in the paragraph below.

Earth's place in the universe has over the 1)_____ of five centuries gone from being at the center of the universe, to being just a dot in a universe filled with billions of galaxies. While we have come to know a great deal about the universe, including how it 2)_____ over time to become what it is today, there is still much we do not know. Everything we know about it is based on just the observable universe, since we cannot know what 3)_____ beyond what our instruments can observe. This means that the universe may be 4)_____ vast, or it may be part of a multiverse that features countless other universes. We will likely never find out, unfortunately, just how big the universe really is, but this 5)_____ can help foster a sense of wonder for us when we look up at the sky at night.

Discussion

Write a short response to the question below. Be prepared to discuss your answer out loud with fellow students if your instructor asks you to do so.

Is it a good idea to send signals from Earth that could theoretically be picked up by alien civilizations? Please explain your answer.

....

....

....

🌐 Point of Interest

Astronomers broke the "cosmic distance record" in 2016 when they used NASA's Hubble Space Telescope, named after Edwin Hubble, to discover GN-z11, which became the farthest known galaxy from Earth. The light from GN-z11 took 13.4 billion years to reach us, and so the image of GN-z11 in the Hubble Space Telescope is from about four hundred million years after the Big Bang.

The Endgame

Has artificial intelligence surpassed human intelligence?

AI（人工知能）は、私たちの生活の様々な側面に急速に根付いている。AI は人間の知能を凌駕するのかという議論を最もよく表しているのが、ゲームの分野だろう。チェスと碁の２つのゲームを例に、AI がこれまでに成し遂げてきたこと、そして AI が人間の知能を凌駕するにはまだどのくらい先が長いのか見てみよう。

Games like chess provide a great way to test how well artificial intelligence stacks up against human intelligence, for it makes it possible to pit a human's reasoning skills and strategic insight against the computational prowess of the most powerful software..

Image credit: @iStockphoto

Getting Started

To help you connect with this chapter's topic, take a moment to think about the questions below, and then write a short sentence to answer each one.

1. What is your favorite fictional story that deals with artificial intelligence?

   _____

2. How often do you play games against computerized opponents?

   _____

3. Which do you think is better at the game of go: a human go master or AI?

   _____

Reading

1 Artificial Intelligence (AI) is rapidly becoming entrenched in many aspects of everyday life. Ranging from certain features of smartphone technology, for example, to robot butlers delivering items to hotel rooms, just about everyone interacts with AI in one form or another on a daily basis. AI is on the cusp of surpassing human abilities with regard to even some complicated tasks. For instance, though the self-driving car is still in its infancy, it likely will not be long before it becomes far safer than the average human driver. AI is even contributing to medical diagnoses by doing things like interpreting medical imaging data from CT scans and MRI scans. There is one area, however, that perhaps best epitomizes the debate over whether or not AI can surpass human intelligence: games. A closer look at two games in particular, and the massive efforts by tech companies to design programs 15 that can best the top human players, will help us see how far AI has come, and how far it has yet to go before truly surpassing human intelligence.

A hotel's robot butler in an elevator
Image credit: The author

2 In 1996, world chess champion Garry Kasparov defeated an IBM supercomputer named Deep Blue. After losing the first game, Kasparov won three games and tied twice. Though Kasparov won the match, the fact that a computer could 20 actually win even just one game against the best human chess player was stunning. Kasparov wrote a short article in *Time* magazine afterward, and said that the computer's decision to sacrifice a pawn at one point in the first game caught his attention since it did not result in an obvious gain. Kasparov later realized the true extent of Deep Blue's computational prowess, for it had actually calculated every possible move up 25 until six moves later when it took one of Kasparov's pawns. According to Kasparov, the pawn sacrifice is a move that he himself might have made, but from the computer's perspective, it was not a sacrifice since it had already calculated that it would recover by taking one of Kasparov's pawns six moves later.

3 Kasparov exposed the computer's limitations in the following games by 30 **adjusting**[1] his style of play and varying his strategy in ways that Deep Blue could not counteract. In effect, even though the computer had an immense database from which to calculate possible moves and possible outcomes, it lacked the ability to learn and adapt beyond the information it already had in its database. The following year, however, Deep Blue, which underwent improvements, stunned the world by winning 35 the match against Kasparov with two wins, three draws, and one loss. For the first time ever, a computer won a match against a world chess champion. According to IBM, Deep Blue had the ability to consider up to two hundred million chess positions per second, and so it appears that sheer computational ability was able to overcome human reasoning.

47 **CD**

5　**4** Chess has long served as an ideal test for artificial intelligence since it requires strategic thinking and, despite its simplistic appearance, it features more possible outcomes than can be programmed. The game of go, however, is even more complex, and so it has proven far more challenging to design a program that can defeat the world's best go players. About twenty years after Deep Blue's

10　victory over Kasparov in chess, a company named DeepMind, which is part of Google's parent company Alphabet Inc., created a program called AlphaGo. This program initially

> チェスと囲碁がどれ
> ほど複雑なのか、章
> 末の Point of Interest
> を読んでみよう。

learned to play by analyzing thousands of human-played games of go, and it defeated several of the world's best go players in matches from 2015 to 2017. Its successor,

15　AlphaGo Zero, was even more impressive insofar as it actually taught itself how to win. It had no input data from previously played games of go, and instead played against itself repeatedly. Within forty days, according to DeepMind, it surpassed every previous version of AlphaGo, and thereby arguably became the strongest player in the world for the game of go.

48 **CD**

20　**5** It is clear that artificial intelligence is rapidly overtaking humans in straightforward games with fixed rules and clear objectives. Kasparov raised a probing question in his *Time* article: if the computer makes the same move as he would, but for different reasons, is it actually an "intelligent" move? Answering Kasparov's question is difficult, since there is a certain degree of **ambiguity**[2] in what "intelligent" means when

25　considered in this more philosophical context. Though AI can process data and even adapt in order to achieve set goals by using algorithms that produce results similar to what the human mind would produce, it cannot experience what it processes. It is not aware of itself or its role in the game. In chess, for instance, it has no will to win, only a programmed objective. It has no fear of defeat, only a set of calculations designed to

30　minimize the probability of losing. Nevertheless, it is clear that rapid advances in AI may one day result in a form of general intelligence capable of out-performing humans in most fields, and perhaps one day it may even be possible for AI to possess something **akin**[3] to a will of its own. It is therefore evident that even though AI has overtaken human intelligence in a few areas, it has not fully surpassed human intelligence yet—

35　but it remains to be seen how much longer this will hold true.

Vocabulary

Use the context in the reading section to figure out the meaning of each underlined word below.

1. … by **adjusting** his style of play …
    a. fixing   b. creating   c. modifying   d. envisioning

2. … there is a certain degree of **ambiguity** in …
    a. truth   b. clarity   c. certainty   d. vagueness

3. … possess something **akin** to a will …
    a. similar   b. including   c. relative   d. considering

Comprehension

Read each statement below carefully, and then based on the information presented in this chapter, write "T" if it is true or "F" if it is false.

1. _____ Garry Kasparov won the match against an IBM computer in 1996, but he lost the first game.

2. _____ The IBM computer Deep Blue won the match against Kasparov in 1997, even though it lost one game.

3. _____ A company named AlphaGo created the computer program DeepMind to play go against the top human players.

4. _____ Go is much more complex than chess, and so far, no computer program can defeat any of the top human go players.

5. _____ The author argues that what makes AI so good at games like chess is that AI cannot experience what it processes, and does not feel fear.

Summary

Listen carefully to the audio recording for this section and fill in the blanks in the paragraph below.

Artificial intelligence, or simply AI, has become an 1)_____ common part of life, and it is now even taking over complex tasks like driving cars. As AI continues to grow in complexity and ability, it is 2)_____ to question whether it is actually on the verge of surpassing human intelligence. One of the most straightforward ways to test AI against human intelligence is by 3)_____ of games like chess and go. A computer program first defeated a human chess world champion in 1997, and a program named AlphaGo Zero has likely 4)_____ the best go player in the world. Though AI can beat humans in strategic games with defined rules, and even take on complex tasks like driving cars, it still does not show signs of consciousness, and so it does not appear that AI will 5)_____ surpass human intelligence any time soon.

Discussion

Write a short response to the question below. Be prepared to discuss your answer out loud with fellow students if your instructor asks you to do so.

How comfortable are you with the idea of riding in a car that uses artificial intelligence to drive itself? Please explain your answer.

....

....

....

🌐 Point of Interest

It has been said that there are more possible ways for a game of chess to play out, based on the multiple ways two players can move their pieces, than there are atoms in the observable universe. The game of go, however, is even more complex. In fact, according to the company DeepMind, the game of go is a googol, which is a one followed by a hundred zeroes, times more complex than chess.

Heads Up

Could a large asteroid wipe out mankind?

地球には宇宙空間からの砕片が絶えず衝突している。幸いなことに、大気圏に突入する物体の大半は危害を与えず地球の表面に衝突するはるか前に燃え尽き、地表にまで到達する物体は通常小さくて大して被害を与えない。しかし、恐竜を根絶させたと多くの人が考えている小惑星のような大きい物体が地球に衝突することもあり得るだろう。巨大隕石が落下する危険性は高いのか、また何らかの防御策はあるのだろうか。

This famous meteorite impact crater in Arizona is a little over a kilometer in diameter and about 170 meters deep, and was created when an asteroid struck approximately fifty thousand years ago.

Image credit: The author

Getting Started

To help you connect with this chapter's topic, take a moment to think about the questions below, and then write a short sentence to answer each one.

1. How many shooting stars have you seen in your lifetime?

   _____

2. What is your favorite fictional story that deals with outer space?

   _____

3. How worried are you about the possibility of an asteroid striking on Earth?

   _____

Reading

1 If you stare at the night sky long enough, away from city lights, you will likely see what is sometimes colloquially referred to as a shooting star. What people often refer to as a shooting star is actually a meteor, which is a meteoroid that emits bright light as it burns up while streaking through our atmosphere. Occasionally, meteors
5 qualify as bolides or even superbolides, which are especially bright meteors that tend to explode in the atmosphere. In 2013, one superbolide was so bright that it was plainly visible in daylight as it streaked across the morning sky over Chelyabinsk, Russia. It then exploded about fifty kilometers above the surface, and created a sonic blast that destroyed thousands of windows and resulted in over a thousand injuries. The dramatic
10 video footage of this incident serves as a stark reminder that our planet is vulnerable to threats from above. Let us therefore examine this topic further to see how serious the threat is, and what is being done to help protect us.

2 Bright city lights make it difficult to see a meteor streaking across the sky in urban areas, except perhaps during events like the Perseids meteor shower that
15 annually peaks in August. Nevertheless, even though we may not be able to see them, countless bits of space dust and meteoroids enter Earth's atmosphere every day. Some meteoroids survive the journey through the atmosphere, and what remains of those that strike Earth's surface are called meteorites. While meteoroids are typically quite small and usually do not pose much of a threat to people, larger asteroid **fragments**[1]
20 or whole asteroids do occasionally strike Earth. According to the National Aeronautics and Space Administration (NASA), objects capable of causing damage to the impact area strike Earth approximately once every two thousand years, while an object large enough to pose a serious threat to life on Earth strikes only once every few million years.

25 **3** There is no better example of the danger that large asteroids pose to life than the one that **slammed**[2] into Earth approximately sixty-six million years ago. This asteroid was at least ten kilometers in diameter, and upon impact with Earth's surface it created a huge crater known as
30 the Chicxulub crater, which lies beneath the Yucatán Peninsula in Mexico. The damage from such a massive impact was absolutely catastrophic, for it triggered earthquakes that may have reached
35 eleven on the Richter scale, and the particles from the impact that were

Tyrannosaurus rex, one of the last dinosaur species
Image credit: The author

spewed up into the atmosphere likely reduced the amount of sunlight that reached the surface, which disrupted the ecosystem. This impact is widely believed to have coincided with one of the most notable mass extinction events in Earth's history, which resulted in about seventy-five percent of plant and animal species going extinct, including most dinosaur species. Needless to say, the prospect of another large asteroid 5 like this striking our planet in the future is a serious concern.

53 CD

4 Various space agencies around the world are working on ways to identify threats to our planet from things like asteroids. For example, NASA, which has long been at the forefront of space projects, has established the Near-Earth Object (NEO) Observations Program, which looks for NEOs that come within about fifty million 10 kilometers of Earth's orbit. As a member of the International Asteroid Warning Network, which is sanctioned by the United Nations, NASA coordinates its efforts to identify potential threats to our planet with the efforts of other countries. NASA is also working on ways to actually ward off potential future asteroid strikes. For example, it is directing the Double Asteroid Redirection Test (DART) mission, which will test the 15 effectiveness of using spacecraft as kinetic impactors. This involves sending a spacecraft that will impact a small asteroid, which is actually in orbit around a larger asteroid named Didymos. The DART spacecraft is scheduled to reach its target in the fall of 2022, at which time it will become clearer how effective a kinetic impactor can be for the purpose of altering an asteroid's trajectory. 20

54 CD

5 Ultimately, the threat of an asteroid strike is relatively minor in comparison with more **urgent**[3] problems in the world right now, including climate change, pollution, and the destruction of natural habitats. Many astronomers, however, believe that when it comes to a large asteroid strike, it is not a question of if, but when, and unfortunately it is clear that we 25 are not yet ready to face such a threat. Kinetic impactors, for example, require one to two years of warning time to deal with small asteroids, which may be reasonable. When it comes to

> この火球と同じ日に
> 地球に近づいた小惑
> 星について、章末
> の Point of Interest
> を読んでみよう。

a large asteroid, however, decades of advance warning time may be necessary in order to effectively alter its trajectory so that it safely avoids Earth. The bottom line is that 30 there is always the possibility that a particularly large asteroid, or even a comet, could make its way to Earth before we have developed the needed capabilities to prevent it from striking our planet's surface. Fortunately, dedicated space agencies around the world are formulating strategies that will hopefully be in place long before an especially menacing threat from above reaches Earth. 35

···

meteor「流星」 meteoroid「流星体」 streak「流星のように走る」 bolide「火球」 superbolide「大火球」 sonic「音速の」 blast「爆風」 stark「明確な」 Perseids「ペルセウス座流星群」 meteorite「隕石（いんせき）」 asteroid「小惑星」 Chicxulub crater「チチュルブクレーター」 Richter scale「リクター・スケール」 spew「噴出する」 Near-Earth Object Observations Program「地球近傍天体観測計画」 International Asteroid Warning Network「国際小惑星警報ネットワーク」 Double Asteroid Redirection Test「二重小惑星軌道変更計画」 kinetic「動的」 impactor「衝撃装置」 Didymos「ディディモス」 trajectory「軌道」

Vocabulary

Use the context in the reading section to figure out the meaning of each underlined word below.

1. … larger asteroid **fragments** or whole asteroids …
   - a. pieces
   - b. functions
   - c. trails
   - d. cores

2. … the one that **slammed** into Earth …
   - a. crashed
   - b. arrived
   - c. landed
   - d. reached

3. … in comparison with more **urgent** problems …
   - a. strange
   - b. pressing
   - c. alert
   - d. rare

Comprehension

Read each statement below carefully, and then based on the information presented in this chapter, write "T" if it is true or "F" if it is false.

1. _____ In 2013, a large meteor known as a superbolide crashed on Russian land and damaged thousands of windows.

2. _____ An object able to threaten life on Earth strikes only once every few million years according to NASA.

3. _____ It is widely believed that a large asteroid is responsible for the extinction of dinosaurs millions of years ago.

4. _____ DART will be tested to see if kinetic impactors could help safeguard Earth from asteroids.

5. _____ According to the author, since large asteroids strike Earth only every few million years, there is no rush to prepare for an asteroid strike.

Summary

Listen carefully to the audio recording for this section and fill in the blanks in the paragraph below.

Earth is constantly getting struck by debris from space, 1)_____ from bits of space dust, to larger objects like asteroid fragments that burn up as they enter our atmosphere. Fortunately, the vast majority of objects that enter our atmosphere are 2)_____ and burn up long before striking our planet's surface. Although the objects that do make it to the surface are usually too small to cause much damage, a few rare ones are large enough to 3)_____ pose a risk to everything in the impact area. The real concern, however, is that a large asteroid like the one that many believe is 4)_____ for wiping out the dinosaurs could one day strike our planet. Space agencies around the world are therefore taking this threat seriously by 5)_____ the skies for such objects, and coming up with ways to defend against them.

Discussion

Write a short response to the question below. Be prepared to discuss your answer out loud with fellow students if your instructor asks you to do so.

How do you think society would react if a huge asteroid heading for Earth could not be stopped? Please explain your answer.

....

....

....

🌐 Point of Interest

On the same day that a superbolide streaked over Russia in 2013, Asteroid 2012 DA14, later named 367943 Duende, came within just 27,700 kilometers of Earth. To get a sense of just how close it was to our planet, consider the following distances. Earth is 147,000,000 kilometers away from the Sun at perihelion, which is the point in Earth's orbit when it is closest to the Sun. The distance between Earth and the Moon is just over 363,000 kilometers at perigee, which is the point in the Moon's orbit when it is closest to Earth. Much closer still, communications and weather satellites in geostationary orbit are 36,000 kilometers from our planet's surface.

Destination Mars

When will humans first set foot on the Red Planet?

宇宙探査時代の最大の功績は月面着陸であったが、近い将来に火星への有人飛行がこれをしのぐかもしれない。現在いくつかの国と私企業が火星に人間を送り出す計画を立てているが、克服すべきいくつかの障害もある。赤い惑星に人類が足を踏み入れるのはいつごろになるだろうか。

The planet Mars is home to Valles Marineris, which is visible in the middle of the image on the right. It is a huge canyon like Arizona's Grand Canyon, except that this Martian canyon is nearly four times as long, about twenty times as wide, and up to nearly five times as deep.

Image credit: NASA

Getting Started

To help you connect with this chapter's topic, take a moment to think about the questions below, and then write a short sentence to answer each one.

1. Would you be willing to go on a one-way trip to Mars?

   _____

2. What is your favorite fictional story about Mars?

   _____

3. When do you think humans will first land on Mars?

   _____

Reading

56

1 Exploration is an essential feature of human existence, and so it is no surprise that the rapid advances in technology in the twentieth century led mankind to embark on ambitious space exploration programs. Beginning in 1957 with a Soviet satellite named *Sputnik*, space exploration has since then blossomed, featuring accomplishments that include sending satellites to the edge of our solar system, landing spacecraft on 5 Mars, and having men walk on the Moon. Landing on the Moon has long been the pinnacle achievement of the space exploration era, but manned missions to Mars may soon eclipse this accomplishment. As exciting as it is to think about watching the first person set foot on Mars, the reality is that many **obstacles**[1] still stand in the way of this goal. Let us therefore take a closer look at this topic to figure out when we can expect 10 to see humans finally set foot on the Red Planet.

57

2 The journey to Mars began in 1964, when the National Aeronautics and Space Administration (NASA) launched *Mariner 4*, which made its closest approach to Mars on July 15, 1965, and in the process became the first spacecraft to successfully complete a flyby of the Red Planet. Another step along the journey to Mars came in 1971, when NASA's *Mariner 9* became the first spacecraft to enter orbit around Mars. Then, in 1976, NASA's *Viking 1* became the first spacecraft to land on Mars. After a relatively uneventful twenty years of Mars exploration following *Viking 1*, NASA's *Mars Pathfinder* landed on the Red Planet on July 4, 1997, and unloaded the first rover, named *Sojourner*, to explore

Sojourner on the surface of Mars
Image credit: NASA/JPL

15

20

25

the Martian surface. Multiple unmanned missions to Mars have since been launched, including NASA's *InSight* lander, which touched down on the planet's surface in 2018.

58

3 Mars is undoubtedly the most **suitable**[2] planet for human exploration and settlement. Earth's other immediate neighbor, Venus, is actually closer, but it is far too inhospitable. Surface temperatures reach 470 degrees Celsius, and the atmosphere is so 30 dense that standing on the surface of Venus is the equivalent of being approximately 1.6 kilometers under water on Earth. The few probes sent to the surface of Venus remained functional for just a matter of hours. Surface conditions on Mars are also quite inhospitable, but not nearly as harsh as those on Venus. Mars has an average temperature of minus sixty-three degrees Celsius, with lows of minus 140 degrees 35 and highs of thirty degrees, and its atmosphere is a hundred times thinner than

Earth's. Though such an environment obviously cannot support human life, we have the technology needed to make spacesuits and build bases that can withstand such conditions.

59 CD

4 How likely is it, then, that we will see a manned mission to Mars in the foreseeable future? American President Donald Trump signed Space Policy Directive 1 in 2017, which outlines a plan for NASA to establish a lunar base and then use that as a starting point for a manned mission to Mars, in collaboration with the private sector. Ideally, this could lead to a successful launch of a manned mission to Mars in the 2030s. Several companies, however, ambitiously aim to put humans on Mars sometime in the 2020s. The recent wave of successful unmanned Mars missions makes it seem like these timeframes are technically possible, but preparing for such missions could end up taking longer than **anticipated**[3] since finding a way to safely transport humans and necessary supplies to the Red Planet is a major challenge. The journey to Mars with current space travel capabilities typically takes about six months, so the psychological toll of being confined in a small spacecraft for such a long journey is a serious concern. Additionally, it takes approximately three to twenty-two minutes for radio signals to travel between Earth and Mars, depending on how far apart the planets are, which means that astronauts heading to Mars will be cut off from real-time communication. Further complicating things is that the distance between Earth and Mars varies dramatically as they orbit the Sun, and so spacecraft can only launch for a brief period of time every two years.

60 CD

5 Ultimately, it seems certain that space agencies will overcome these challenges and land humans on Mars sometime in the next few decades. Whether or not we will also see permanent human settlements soon after, though, is less clear. The Moon landings can serve as a warning against setting expectations too high for the colonization of Mars. When the *Apollo 11* mission's lunar module *Eagle* landed on the Moon on July 20, 1969, and Neil Armstrong became the first human to walk on the Moon, some people back on Earth envisioned that lunar colonies would soon be established. However, NASA astronauts landed on the Moon only five more times after the *Apollo 11* mission, the last time being in 1972, and to this day only twelve men have walked on the Moon. Regardless of when humans do end up getting to Mars, expanding our presence to another planet will clearly have a profound effect on the course of human history, and it will transform the world as we know it. In this way, then, discussions about manned missions to the Red Planet and potential settlements on its surface serve as sure signs that human beings collectively truly are getting ready to change the world.

NASA の火星探査計画で使用された探査機（ローバー）について、章末の Point of Interest を読んでみよう。

embark on「開始する」 Sputnik「スプートニク」 spacecraft「宇宙船」 pinnacle「頂点」 manned mission「有人飛行」 eclipse「しのぐ」 Red Planet「赤い惑星（火星の俗称）」 flyby「（天体への）接近通過」 Mariner 9「マリナー９号」 Mars Pathfinder「火星パスファインダー」 unload「降ろす」 Sojourner「ソジャーナ」 InSight「インサイト (*Interior* Exploration using *Seismic* Investigations, *Geodesy* and *Heat Transport*)」 lander「着陸船」 atmosphere「大気」 Venus「金星」 low「最低気温」 high「最高温度」 withstand「に耐える」 feasible「実行可能な」 habitat「生息地」 toll「痛手，代償」 orbit「（天体の）周りを軌道を描いて回る」 Space Policy Directive 1「宇宙政策指令１」 foreseeable「予測可能な」 lunar「月の」 timeframe「（予定の）期間，時間枠」 colonization「入植」 Apollo 11「アポロ11号」 lunar module「月着陸船」 Neil Armstrong「ニール・アームストロング（1930-2012）」 envision「予見する」

Vocabulary

Use the context in the reading section to figure out the meaning of each underlined word below.

1. … many **obstacles** still stand in the way …

    a. opportunities   b. barriers   c. tragedies   d. changes

2. … the most **suitable** planet for human exploration …

    a. beautiful   b. interesting   c. satisfactory   d. challenging

3. … taking longer than **anticipated** since …

    a. expected   b. feared   c. discussed   d. motivated

Comprehension

Read each statement below carefully, and then based on the information presented in this chapter, write "T" if it is true or "F" if it is false.

1. _____ After *Viking 1* became the first spacecraft to land on Mars, NASA immediately launched many additional significant missions to Mars.

2. _____ The surface of Venus is covered in water that is approximately 1.6 kilometers deep.

3. _____ There have been multiple unmanned missions to Mars in the two decades since NASA's *Mars Pathfinder* landed on the planet in 1997.

4. _____ Transporting humans to Mars would be easy, but it is not yet possible to make spacesuits that can support life on Mars.

5. _____ According to the author, we should not assume that settlements will automatically follow the first manned mission to Mars.

Summary

Listen carefully to the audio recording for this section and fill in the blanks in the paragraph below.

Mars is clearly the best choice when it comes to launching manned missions to 1)_____ planet, since it is the only one in our solar system with mild enough conditions. Beginning in 1964, NASA has launched spacecraft that have 2)_____ close to Mars, orbited it, landed on it, and even delivered rovers to explore its surface. There are now 3)_____ to send humans to Mars, and various countries and private companies have different timeframes for when they hope to land humans on the Red Planet. When it comes to the issue of humans 4)_____ foot on Mars, one thing seems certain: it is not a question of if, but rather, when. Seeing humanity's 5)_____ on another planet will surely affect the way most people see the world, and so discussions about manned missions to Mars indicate that humanity is truly getting ready to change the world.

Discussion

Write a short response to the question below. Be prepared to discuss your answer out loud with fellow students if your instructor asks you to do so.

If you had an opportunity to go to Mars, would you be willing to leave Earth for several years? Please explain your answer.

....

....

....

🌐 Point of Interest

The *Mars Pathfinder* mission's rover, named *Sojourner*, became a bit of a celebrity the moment the first images of it on the Martian surface came back to Earth. *Sojourner* made the July 14, 1997, cover of *Time* magazine, and even featured somewhat prominently in two popular Hollywood movies: *Red Planet* and *The Martian*.

Selected Bibliography

The following sources were helpful while writing this book, and may therefore also prove beneficial for students who are interested in learning more about some of the topics covered in the preceding chapters.

Allcott, Hunt, and Matthew Gentzkow. "Social Media and Fake News in the 2016 Election." *Journal of Economic Perspectives* 31, No. 2 (Spring 2017): 211-236.

Bernstein, Jacob. "The Price French Bulldogs Pay for Being So Cute." *The New York Times*, March 16, 2018.

Carroll, Sean. *The Big Picture: On the Origins of Life, Meaning, and the Universe Itself.* New York: Dutton, 2016.

Chase, M.J., S. Schlossberg, C.R. Griffin, P.J.C. Bouché, S.W. Djene, P.W. Elkan, S. Ferreira, et al. (2016). "Continent-wide survey reveals massive decline in African savannah elephants." *PeerJ* 4:e2354, https://doi.org/10.7717/peerj.2354.

Cox, Brian, and Jeff Forshaw. *The Quantum Universe (and why anything that can happen, does).* Boston: Da Capo Press, 2011.

Bieler, Des. "Brett Favre says he suffered 'probably thousands' of concussions." *The Washington Post*, April 12, 2018.

Dallaire, Roméo. *Shake Hands with the Devil: The Failure of Humanity in Rwanda.* New York: Carroll & Graf Publishers, 2003.

de Soete, François. "The Nuclear Non-Proliferation Regime: Trying to Maintain the Status Quo." In *Security and Defence: National and International Issues,* edited by Keane Grimsrud, 66-77. Kingston, Ontario: 2003.

de Soete, Francois, et al. "The President versus the Press: Analyzing President Trump's Fake News Awards." *Ritsumeikan Social Sciences Review* 55, no. 1 (June 2019): 303-317.

Doudna, Jennifer A., and Samuel H. Sternberg. *A Crack in Creation: Gene Editing and the Unthinkable Power to Control Evolution.* New York: Houghton Mifflin Harcourt Publishing Company, 2017.

Greene, Brian. *The Elegant Universe: Superstrings, Hidden Dimensions, and the Quest for the Ultimate Theory.* New York: W. W. Norton & Company, Inc., 1999.

Greene, Brian. *The Fabric of the Cosmos: Space, Time, and the Texture of Reality.* New York: Vintage Books, Inc., 2004.

Greene, Brian. *The Hidden Reality: Parallel Universes and Deep Laws of the Cosmos.* New York: Vintage Books, Inc., 2011.

Hawking, Stephen. *A Brief History of Time: From the Big Bang to Black Holes.* New York: Bantam Books, 1988.

Hawking, Stephen, and Leonard Mlodinow. *The Grand Design.* New York: Bantam Books, 2010.

Hetherington, Mike. "Farber: Kariya has no memory of Game 6, 'it's pretty frightening.'" *TSN.ca*, September 27, 2017. https://www.tsn.ca/farber-kariya-never-the-same-after-suter-hit-1.868651

International Air Transport Association. "Traveler Numbers Reach New Heights: IATA World Air Transport Statistics Released." *Press Release* No. 51, September 6, 2018. https://www.iata.org/pressroom/pr/Pages/2018-09-06-01.aspx

IPBES. *Summary for policymakers of the global assessment report on biodiversity and ecosystem services of the Intergovernmental Science-Policy Platform on Biodiversity and Ecosystem Services.* Edited by S. Díaz, J. Settele, E. S. Brondizio., H. T. Ngo, M. Guèze, J. Agard, A. Arneth, et al. Bonn, Germany: IPBES Secretariat, 2019.

Kasparov, Garry. "The Day that I sensed a New Kind of Intelligence." *Time*, March 25, 1996.

Kruger, Justin, and David Dunning. "Unskilled and Unaware of It: How Difficulties in Recognizing One's Own Incompetence Lead to Inflated Self-Assessments." *Journal of Personality and Social Psychology* 77, No. 6 (1999): 1121-1134.

Kristensen, Hans M., and Matt Korda. "Status of World Nuclear Forces." *Federation of American Scientists*, May 2019. https://fas.org/issues/nuclear-weapons/status-world-nuclear-forces/

Omalu, Bennet. *Truth Doesn't Have a Side: My Alarming Discovery about the Danger of Contact Sports.* Grand Rapids, MI: Zondervan, 2017.

Packer, Craig, Dennis Ikanda, Bernard Kissui, and Hadas Kushnir. "Lion Attacks on Humans in Tanzania." *Nature* 436 (2005): 927-928.

Reid, Carlton. "All New Cars to Have Speed Limiters Fitted, Rules European Parliament." *Forbes*, February 27, 2019.

Sandel, Michael J. *The Case against Perfection: Ethics in the Age of Genetic Engineering.* Cambridge, MA: Belknap Press, 2007.

Shelley, Mary. *Frankenstein: The 1818 Text.* New York: Penguin Books, 2018.

Stannard, Russell. *The End of Discovery: Are We Approaching the Boundaries of the Knowable?* Oxford: Oxford University Press, 2010.

Sullivan, Sidney. "Map: Fatal Bear Attacks in North America." *KTTU-TV Anchorage*, July 5, 2017. https://www.ktuu.com/content/news/MAP-Fatal-Bear-Attacks-in-North-America-432734333.html.

Taylor, Alex, III. "10 Ways Germans Rule the Road." *CNN*, June 20, 2012. https://money.cnn.com/galleries/2012/autos/1206/gallery.german-cars.fortune/4.html

United Nations World Tourism Association. "International Tourist Arrivals Reach 1.4 Billion Two Years Ahead of Forecasts." *Press Release* No. 19003, January 21, 2019. http://www2.unwto.org/press-release/2019-01-21/international-tourist-arrivals-reach-14-billion-two-years-ahead-forecasts

TEXT PRODUCTION STAFF

edited by	編集
Kimio Sato	佐藤 公雄

English-language editing by	英文校閲
Bill Benfield	ビル・ベンフィールド

cover design by	表紙デザイン
Ruben Frosali	ルーベ ン・フロサリ

text design by	本文デザイン
Ruben Frosali	ルーベ ン・フロサリ

CD PRODUCTION STAFF

recorded by	吹き込み者
Lindsay Nelson (AmerE)	リンジー・ネルソン（アメリカ英語）
Bob Werley (AmerE)	ボブ・ワーリー（アメリカ英語）

Getting Ready to Change the World
－New Challenges, New Opportunities－
グローバル時代を生き抜く変革への視点

2020年1月20日　初版発行
2023年3月10日　第6刷発行

著　　者　François de Soete

編 註 者　浪田 克之介

発 行 者　佐野 英一郎

発 行 所　株式会社 成 美 堂
　　　　　〒101-0052　東京都千代田区神田小川町3-22
　　　　　TEL 03-3291-2261　FAX 03-3293-5490
　　　　　https://www.seibido.co.jp

印刷・製本　（株）加藤文明社

ISBN 978-4-7919-7212-8　　　　　　　　　　　Printed in Japan